THE ESAU EFFECT

RESHAPING THE WORLD IN THE ACT OF WAR

MICHAEL RAY LEMONS

Copyright @ 2023 by O'Lemon & Underwood Publishing

No part of this publication may be reproduced, distributed, or transmitted in any form or by any means, including photocopying, recording, or other electronic or mechanical methods, without the prior written permission of the publisher, except as permitted by U.S. copyright law.

ISBN: 9798988530312 (Paperback)
ISBN: 9798988530329 (Hardcover)

Published by:
379 North Oates Street P.O. Box 95
Dothan, Alabama 36302

To the memory of Shermaine Jackson. You touched so many hearts with laughter and happiness. Gone but not forgotten.

PREFACE

In this captivating journey, we'll explore the powerful influences of birthrights, ideological contradictions, insatiable greed, and ever-changing borders that have shaped countless human conflicts throughout history. This book aims to reconnect readers with age-old wisdom while simultaneously examining the perplexing question of how ordinary individuals can be swayed to support wide-scale tragedies, corruption, atrocities, and occupation - actions that continue to shape our world today. This enthralling book might stir debate, yet its purpose is to shed light on the ongoing battles of humankind throughout history.

> Then the seventh Angel sounded: And there were loud voices in heaven, saying, "The kingdoms of this world have become the kingdoms of our Lord and His Christ, and He shall reign forever and ever!"
>
> (Rev. 11:15)

ACKNOWLEDGMENTS

It's an honor to collaborate with O'lemon & Underwood Publishing's visionary minds on my account of Esau and the historical events within the Afro-Asiatic and Hamitic regions, illuminating a deep-rooted trail of blood. Growing up in public schools, Africa was depicted as a land of uncivilized, barbaric people. I vividly recall the curriculum during desegregation, which portrayed African black individuals as sub-human and primitive. To think our teachers fed us such falsehoods! The western world has always grappled with the truth.

As I work in the technical sector, I remain inspired by the extraordinary legacies of our ancestors, as well as contemporary leaders and activists pushing for change in policies tied to systemic racism. This continuous struggle for existence deserves immense recognition for its impact on fostering peace, love, and equality.

TABLE OF CONTENTS

Preface iv

Acknowledgments v

CHAPTER 1
Esau: The Genesis of Jealousy, Revenge,
and Uneasy Promise of Peace 1

Chapter 2
Jacob and Esau: The Beginning of a Rivalry.............. 5

CHAPTER 3
"The African Origins of the Hebrew People" 12

CHAPTER 4
The Clash of Civilizations 20

CHAPTER 5
The Imperialist Powers 32

CHAPTER 6
A Devastating Impact on European and
African Economies and Communities 42

CHAPTER 7
The Aftermath 59

CHAPTER 8
The Caste of Supremacy: The Causes of Esau
and Jacob's Conflict in the Modern World 73

Conclusion 84

Bibliography 87

CHAPTER 1

ESAU: THE GENESIS OF JEALOUSY, REVENGE, AND UNEASY PROMISE OF PEACE

More recently, varying cultures have blamed world violence on the courageous Esau, ancestor of the Edomites. Esau was a person of the field with rough virtues favored by his father, Isaac, and vilified by his religious and political enemies. In the biblical narrative, Esau is depicted as a trustworthy, reliable, and diligent individual. However, his most notable downfall was his reckless regard for his birthright, which he traded for a single meal. This act set off a chain of events, fueled by Jacob's cunning deception, that led to ongoing tension between not only the twin brothers but also their future generations.

In the Hebrew faith, one's birthright involves receiving their father's blessing and estate. But it's more than just that being Isaac's firstborn meant inheriting a divine blessing through a sacred covenant. Esau, burning with rage, vowed to slay his sibling, Jacob after their father passed away. However, as time went on, the brothers mended their relationship and laid their past disputes to rest.

During the two global wars, over a hundred million lives were lost across the world, as nations fought for territories in Africa and the Middle East. These devastating battles spanned from the Atlantic and Pacific Islands to the African steppes and Mesopotamian plains. Between May 1914 and the second atomic bomb drop on Nagasaki on August 9, 1945, no other period in history, aside from the Middle Passage, witnessed such immense bloodshed. The aftermath saw the United States and the Soviet Union locked in a race to develop even more potent nuclear weapons, built to deter potential preemptive attacks.

Throughout the Cold War, the United States and the Soviet Union found themselves in a tense and uncertain geopolitical struggle. This pressure led to the formation of alliances like the North Atlantic Treaty Organization (NATO) and the Warsaw Pact. Much like a contagious wave, European hostilities spilled over into other parts of the world as nations vied for economic control and ideological influence. Interestingly, this mirrored the aggressive tactics of Indo-European dominance during Joshua's time.

The Indo-Aryans conquered the territory of the Cushite people who lived in the southwestern region of Arabia and ruthlessly destroyed their settlements. They established settlements, carrying their polytheistic religious system with them and luring the local Hamites into a cult-like way of life as they did so.

The Israelites and African kinfolks formed an alliance under the leadership of Joshua and waged war against the Indo-Aryans and chased them along the road to Beth Horon.

The inhabitants of the heavily fortified twin cities Upper and Lower Beth Horon fled as far as Azekah, where the Lord rained large hailstones from heaven.

> *The Lord commanded the sun to stand still over Gibeon and the moon to stop over the Valley of Aijalon until the people avenged their enemies*
> (Josh:10:10).

Adolf Hitler's massacre of six million Jews, as horrifying as it was, doesn't compare to the one hundred million kidnapped African victims and estimated seventy million deaths during the Black Holocaust of the Middle Passage. So many nearly forgotten horrors, including the uranium gun-type atomic bomb (Little Boy), dropped on Hiroshima in August 1945, followed by a plutonium implosion-type bomb (Fat Man) released on Nagasaki during World War II. This disaster resulted in Japan's unconditional capitulation, which was broadcast over public radio on the 15th of August, 1945, at 10:30 in the morning. On September 2, 1945, at Tokyo time, Japan signed the instrument of surrender, making her surrender effective.

Throughout history, an invisible battle has raged between demonic forces and the angels of Almighty God, splitting the world into 'Good and Evil.'

Through the perspective of our educational system, Africans were portrayed as savages, while Anglo-Saxons were seen as bringing the benefits of Christianity to Africa. This mindset, which placed European civilization on a pedestal and justified dominating other cultures, downplayed the impact of genocides on Africans and other people of color. The western education system used this reasoning to defend the Transatlantic and East African slave trades, as well as colonial ambitions in Africa. Many history books have overlooked Africa's contributions or intentionally destroyed crucial records on Asian and African civilizations.

Esau, an important figure in Abraham's family tree and the founding father of the Edomites, is renowned for his jealousy, vengeful nature, and shaky peace agreements. From the moment of his birth, his spiritual roots were weakened by worldly influences, resulting in feelings of resentment and envy. Esau's tale embodies the battle against a range of challenges - physical, religious, territorial disputes, treachery, ideologies - and even the invisible forces of darkness in our realm and beyond.

CHAPTER 2

JACOB AND ESAU: THE BEGINNING OF A RIVALRY

The dramatic story begins with the birth of two biblical patriarchs fighting for firstborn rights and becoming the father of the chosen people. Esau, indifferent to the sacred agreement, and Jacob, his mother's beloved son, ignited a fierce rivalry between them as twin brothers. The situation only worsened with Esau's defiance of Isaac and Abraham when he chose to marry women outside of their covenant. Their disapproval of Esau's marriages to these non-believers eventually led him to settle down with a woman from his own family clan.

The Lord chose Jacob over Esau to secure the blessing, setting aside the natural protocol. He specified that the promise to Abraham and Isaac would be given to one of His choices.

> *Lest there be any fornicator or profane person* like Esau, who for one morsel of food sold his birthright, for you know that afterward when he wanted to inherit the blessing, he was rejected, for he found no place for repentance, though he sought it diligently with tears
> (Hebrew 12:16–17).

In Genesis 25, the Edomites took a much broader meaning when Esau married Mahalath, the daughter of Ishmael, and intermingled with the Ishmaelites. Ishmael was the first son of Abraham, born to his wife's maidservant, Hagar, when Abraham was eighty-six. Sarah had difficulties producing an heir and remained childless despite the Lord's promise. Sarah offered her maid to help fulfill God's everlasting covenant:

> "This one shall not be your heir, but one who comes from your own body shall be your heir"
> (Gen. 15:4).

Hagar began to mock Sarah when she became pregnant and teased Sarah about her son being the inheritor of Abraham's estate because Ishmael was Abraham's firstborn. However, jealousy and hatred filled the heart of the two women as Sarah dealt harshly with Hagar. The ordeal became so extreme that Hagar fled into the wilderness of Beersheba toward Shur. Hagar was approached by the Angel of the Lord near a spring on the way to Shur between Kadesh and Bered (south of Palestine). Hagar called the well Beer-Lahai-Roi, the "Well of the Living God Who Sees Me."

The Angel commanded Hagar to return to Sarah and revealed the future of her descendants through Ishmael, would also be a great nation, saying:

> *"Behold, you are with child, and you shall bear a son. You shall call his name Ishmael because the Lord has heard your affliction. He shall be a wild man; his hand shall be against every man. And he shall dwell in the presence of all his brethren"*
>
> (Gen. 16:11–12).

Some scholars believe that Hagar was the daughter of a high-ranking official in the Egyptian government who the Philistines probably captured near Gerar. Hagar could have been given to Abraham and Sarah as a peace offering when they were expelled by Abimelech, an Aryan king who had taken over Gerar, a Philistine town near the Egyptian border.

One sunny day, as 13-year-old Ishmael sat with his father Abraham near their tent, a divine messenger and two men appeared. The angel instructed Abraham to start the practice of circumcising all male children at eight days old, beginning with his own son. Failing to do so would mean breaking a sacred covenant. While sharing a meal beneath a tree, they engaged in lively discussions about Sarah, who would soon become a mother.

When Sarah heard the news, she laughed, saying, "After I have grown old, shall I have pleasure, my lord, being old also?" Abraham fell to the ground and began questioning God about how the promise of prosperity would come at ninety-nine years of age. The Lord responded:

> *Ask for Me, behold, My covenant is with you, and you shall be a father of many nations...I will make you exceedingly fruitful and make nations of you, and kings shall come from you. And I will establish My covenant between Me and you and your descendants after you.*

The story became essential to ratifying the covenant to keep the commandments, and Abraham's offspring will bless all nations of the Earth. The Lord pledged to ensure that the Promised Land would become their inheritance and increase Abraham's lineage across the globe.

Following their meal, the Angel of the Lord and the two divine messengers engaged in a riveting conversation about the destiny of Sodom and Gomorrah. These cities, situated near the Dead Sea on the Jordan River plain, were notorious for their appalling sins. The two angels left Abraham's vicinity and went toward the cities of the plains. Shortly afterward, the Lord revealed to Abraham His intentions of destroying Sodom and Gomorrah by fire and brimstone.

> *Then Abraham pleaded with the Lord that "if it were fifty righteous within the city...to at least ten righteous men found in the city, would not God spare the city"*
> (Genesis 18:16–32).

God declared that he would not destroy the city for the sake of ten righteous people. When not even ten men were found in the city, the two angels came to save Lot and his family during the evening hour. Lot insisted that the two men stay at his house for the night.

The next day, a crowd gathered around Lot's home, intent on capturing the two strangers who had entered. The angels advised Lot to bring his family to the nearby town of Zoar. Despite his efforts, Lot couldn't persuade his sons-in-law to flee, as they believed he was merely jesting. Guided by the angels, Lot, along with his wife and daughters, escaped Sodom. Subsequently, a divine shower of brimstone and fire rained down upon Sodom and Gomorrah from above.

Tensions flared up when Sarah overheard Ishmael scoffing at Isaac. Jealousy towards the elder child mounted, and the ongoing strife between the women troubled Abraham. Infuriated, Sarah demanded that Abraham banish both Hagar and her son Ishmael, asserting that Ishmael would not be an heir alongside Isaac. Sarah became angry and said to Abraham, "Cast out this bondwoman and her son; for the son of this bondwoman shall not be heir to my son Isaac."

Once again, jealousy ignited conflict between the two women. The next morning, Abraham woke up early, packed some bread and a water-filled skin, and sent Hagar and her son on their way. They sought shelter in the harsh wilderness of Beersheba, but soon their supplies dwindled. Desperate to comfort her child, Hagar situated him under a bush and sat opposite him. In a pivotal moment, the Lord heard the boy's cries; an angel emerged and revealed a replenishing well to Hagar's awestruck gaze. Ishmael thrived in the wilds of Paran as a skilled hunter, and it was clear from the Scriptures that God held great affection for him:

> *And for Ishmael, I have heard you, Behold, I have blessed him, and will make him fruitful and multiply him exceedingly. He shall beget twelve princes, and I will make him a great nation*
> (Gen. 17:20).

The rivalry between Isaac and Ishmael ended in this narrative of the Bible, and Abraham also sent Keturah's children and unnamed concubines to the country of the east. The Ishmaelites lived as nomads and settled in the land of Ham or the Cushite's territory of Havilah and as far as Shur, east of Egypt in northern Arabia. Ishmael returned when Abraham died to assist Isaac in burying their father in the cave of Machpelah, a land that Abraham purchased as a burial site in Hebron.

Many experts suggest that the descendants of Hagar and Keturah are related to all Arabian people and the founding of Islam. The history of the Arabian people is greatly intertwined with the region now known as the Middle East, particularly in the context of biblical prophecies from the book of Isaiah. In an astounding revelation, Isaiah Chapter 60 predicts that Islamic nations, as descendants of Keturah and Hagar, will welcome the original Israelites back to their homeland.

The authors of the Bible paint a vivid picture where religion takes a backseat when divine glory triumphs over a global political and economic system led by the antichrist. Neither capitalism nor socialism can compete with God's plan for economic prosperity.

Abraham's beginnings in the southern Mesopotamian city of Ur, near the Euphrates River, hold great significance. This area saw an influx of Indo-Europeans from the Balkan steppes, adding to its historic importance. These newcomers introduced their moon god Sin as the chief deity.

This blending of cultures and open worship of numerous gods prompted Terah to lead his family away from the pagan-infused environment and set out towards Canaan. Sadly, Lot's father Haran passed away before they left Ur of the Chaldeans. Undeterred, Terah helmed the migration southward to Canaan.

However, Terah chose to settle in Haran, a city named after his late son, accompanied by Abraham and his grandson Lot. In a book attributed to him, Joshua gathered people to deliver a speech recounting the Hebrew people's history:

"Then Joshua gathered all the tribes of Israel to Shechem and called for the elders of Israel...Thus says the Lord God of Israel: 'Your fathers, including Terah, the father of Abraham and the father of Nahor, dwell on the other side of the River in old times; and they served other gods. Then I

took your father Abraham from the other side of the River, led him throughout all the land of Canaan, and multiplied his descendants and gave him Isaac. To Isaac, I gave Jacob and Esau. To Esau, I gave the mountains of Seir to possess, but Jacob and his children went down to Egypt.'"
(Joshua 24: 1–3)

In an enthralling episode of history, the European-origin Aryan Hyksos, also referred to as Philistines, embarked on a journey towards Hebron in Mesopotamia. As they traveled, they turned Hebron into a flourishing royal city teeming with activity along a bustling trade route. However, their endeavors were thwarted by the Egyptian navy, driving the Aryans to retreat into Canaan. Undeterred, they continued down the Nile to unite with other tribes of Indo-European lineage.

CHAPTER 3

"THE AFRICAN ORIGINS OF THE HEBREW PEOPLE"

The rivalry continued for control of the plain with a coalition of Aryan tribes that conquered Negeb, the hub that connects Israel's trade routes with Arabia. They established a civilization that extended from Beersheba to Dan until it was wrestled away by Joshua and Caleb during the Exodus from Egypt. The Aryan Hyksos invaded the Hamite territory in southwestern Arabia and savagely burned their cities to the ground. The Hyksos built settlements, bringing along their polytheistic religious system and enticing the Hamites into a cult lifestyle. The Aryan Hyksos took permanent root, intermingling with the Arabian, Egyptian, and Israelite civilizations.

Many believe that Abraham was the pioneer in worshipping the one true God, earning him the title *"Hebrew."* This term has its roots in the name Eber (Genesis 10:21), an ancestor of Abraham hailing from the land 'beyond the River.' The Bible tells us that during Eber's lifetime, the Earth experienced a division after the great flood (Gen. 10: 25). Thus, the term *"Hebrew"* was used to highlight differences among races, and it became a significant moniker for Abraham and his descendants.

"Then I took your father Abraham from the other side of the River, led him throughout all the land of Canaan, and multiplied his descendants and gave him Isaac" (Joshua 24: 3).

You might be surprised to learn that, historically, several Cushite and Arabian tribes spoke Hebrew dialects and worshiped Yahweh, the one true God worthy of devotion. Ezekiel 29 delves into the Hebrew people's origins, pinpointing their birthplace as Aswan, a city nestled along the Nile River in southern Egypt.

Although there are five forms of Judaism today, not all conservative doctrines acknowledge its early development in Africa by African people. The foundation of Judaism lies in the belief in a single God, Yahweh—a faith that recognizes Abraham as the father of numerous nations. Through his lineage, a new covenant was established, giving rise to the nation of Israel.

The well-known story of the Exodus from Egypt led the Israelites to receive divine law on Mount Sinai en route to Canaan, the Promised Land. Moses famously chose to align with his Israelite heritage rather than his ties to Pharaoh's daughter, Hatshepsut. This decision was solidified when he witnessed an Egyptian official mistreating an enslaved Israelite—resulting in Moses taking the life of this oppressor.

Moses fled to Midian for the next forty years. The historian Josephus gives an apparent variant of the Ethiopian version when Moses escaped the wrath of Pharaoh and resided in the land of Midian. Moses married an Ethiopian priest's daughter and became Ethiopia's king for forty years.

Today, Judaism has been adopted and altered by non-Africans, but shares an intricate principle in derivations of Jewish law. The belief in one God, a monotheistic force, represented an African way of life long before the arrival of the Indo-Europeans who believed in many gods, with each deity having its function of dominance.

Terah decided to make Haran his permanent home after arriving there while traveling with his son, Abraham, his daughter-in-law, Sarah, and his grandson, Lot. Terah was inspired by the city of Haran's riches and prosperity.

In the region surrounding Haran, false gods were prevalent, particularly the moon deity close to present-day Altınbaşak, Turkey. Haran, during Abraham's era, served as a bustling hub of trade, intellect, and faith. Situated strategically along the main trading path connecting Nineveh and Carchemish by the Mediterranean Coast, its significance was undeniable. It was in a dream that the Lord spoke to Abraham:

Get out of your country from your family and your father's house to a land I will show you. I will make you a great nation; I will bless you and make your name great; and you shall be a blessing. I will bless those who bless you, and I will curse him who curses you, and in you, all families of the earth shall be blessed
(Gen. 12:12–1).

At the ripe age of seventy-five, Abraham embarked on a journey with his wife Sarah and nephew Lot, taking everything, they owned. Their destination was Canaan, specifically a town named Shechem. Upon reaching Canaan, Abraham experienced an encounter with the Lord. It was in this moment that the Lord confirmed Canaan as the land promised to Abraham's descendants. Filled with gratitude, Abraham built his very first altar to the Lord in this land.

In the ancient city of Shechem, God revealed Himself to Abraham, reaffirming that his descendants, beginning with Isaac, would inherit this very land. At that time, the Canaanites and Perizzites inhabited Israel, eventually becoming the well-known Philistines mentioned in the Bible.

As Abraham journeyed through Canaan, he headed east of Bethel and stationed his tent between Bethel and Ai. In this location, he constructed a second altar dedicated to God. Accompanied by Sarah, Lot, their numerous livestock, and a wealth of silver and gold treasures, they continued their voyage southward towards Egypt. The catalyst for their departure from Canaan was an intense famine, prompting the decision to seek refuge in Egypt.

Before arriving in Egypt, Abraham said to Sarah: "Indeed, I know that you are a beautiful woman of beautiful countenance. Therefore, when the Egyptians see you, it will happen that they will say, 'This is his wife,' and they will kill me, but let you live. Please say you are my sister that it may be well with me for your sake and that I may live because of you" (Gen. 11–13).

Upon arriving in Gerar, a prosperous city near Egypt, Abraham found a vast expanse of land to the east, situated in the desert between Kadesh and Shur. Here, he pitched his tents and tended to his livestock. Word of Sarah's stunning beauty soon reached Abimelech, the king of Gerar. Thanks to Sarah, Abraham received great favor from Abimelech and his wealth grew immensely through increasing numbers of sheep, oxen, donkeys, and camels.

Eventually, the princess of Gerar brought Sarah before the king with intentions of making her a royal concubine. However, divine intervention struck in the form of severe plagues upon Abimelech's household—all due to Sarah's involvement.

The Lord came to Abimelech in a dream and told him that the woman he had taken was a man's wife. But Abimelech points out to the Lord that both Abraham and Sarah told him they were siblings, and he is innocent because of the integrity of his heart and hands. The Lord said to him in the dream:

> *Yes, I know you did this with the integrity of your heart. For I also withheld you from sinning against Me; therefore, I did not let you touch her. Therefore, restore the man's wife; he is a prophet and will pray for you, and you shall live. But if you do not restore her, know that you shall surely die*
>
> (Gen. 20:5–7).

The next day, as Abimelech woke up, he urgently gathered all his servants and shared his mysterious dream. He then confronted Abraham, asking, "What were you thinking when you did this?" Abraham carefully tried to justify his actions in a way that would calm the king. He explained that during those times, the Aryans' brutal custom was to murder husbands and enslave their wives and children, so he had no choice but to be truthful in his response. "I thought surely the fear of God is not in this place, and they will kill me because of my wife. But she is truly my sister. She is my father's daughter, but not my mother's, and she became my wife."

> After Abraham responded, Abimelech said, "See, my land is before you; dwell where it pleases you"
>
> (Gen. 20:15).

Abimelech told Sarah that he had given Abraham a thousand pieces of silver to vindicate her honor. Again, a conflict arose between Abimelech and Abraham over water rights. Abraham had moved farther south toward Beersheba, digging several wells in the desert for grazing their herds. Abimelech's servants seized the well without the king's permission, which brought a rebuke from Abraham.

In the land of Beersheba, before heading back to Canaan, Abraham and his army commander struck an agreement with

Abimelech, who also attended the gathering. During this time, a dispute arose between Abraham's herdsmen and Lot's servants over prime grazing land with access to abundant water. This disagreement led Abraham to offer Lot the first choice of land in the fertile Jordan River valley near Sodom.

With their families and belongings in tow, Abraham and his entourage left Egypt and set off for Canaan. By that point, both Abraham and Lot had amassed vast herds of livestock, leading to tensions between them and the locals of Gerar due to the sheer size of their possessions.

> *After Abraham departed from Lot, the Lord said, "Lift your eyes and look from where you are –northward, southward, and eastward, for all the land which you see I give to you and your descendants forever. And I will make your descendants as the dust of the earth"*
> (Gen. 13:14–16).

In Genesis 14, we witness a fierce battle led by the Elamite king, Chedorlaomer, and his three allies, including the formidable Tidal king of nations. Their violent conquest on Jordan's plain allowed them to dominate the Arabian trade routes leading to Canaan. During this intense conflict, Lot and his family were captured, and all their belongings were seized as war spoils. To further instill fear, Chedorlaomer's forces constructed massive burial pits in the Valley of Siddim for their victims, ensuring the panicked flight of the Sodom and Gomorrah kings.

However, hope emerged with the King of Salem, Melchizedek. With his assistance, Abraham rallied 318 skilled warriors to challenge Chedorlaomer's forces. Employing a strategic nighttime ambush, Abraham's troops caught their enemies off-guard, liberating Lot and his family from captivity. They also recovered all stolen goods and servants. To express gratitude,

Abraham gifted Melchizedek one-tenth of the retrieved possessions as a tithe and acknowledged him as the Priest of God Most High.

In the epic saga of Abraham's lineage, no rivalry could compare to the intense battle between Jacob and Esau. These twins, born to Isaac and Rebekah, started their struggle for dominion within their mother's womb. A divine prophecy declared two nations would arise from her womb, with the elder brother destined to serve the younger. Back in those days, it was customary for the eldest son to receive a lion's share of the family wealth, known as 'birthright.'

In the womb, Jacob and Esau had a fierce struggle, causing Jacob to latch onto Esau's heel during birth. As they grew older, Esau became a rugged and skillful hunter, earning his father's favor. In contrast, his twin brother Jacob developed into a gentle and spiritual person who cared deeply about fulfilling his divine purpose.

Despite this, it was Jacob who won their mother Rebekah's heart. She helped him deceive their nearly blind father into giving him Esau's blessing. This wasn't the first time Jacob had tricked Esau — he'd previously taken advantage of his brother's vulnerability to trade a bowl of stew for Esau's birthright. When the time came to receive their father's blessing, Rebekah dressed Jacob in Esau's clothes and covered his smooth skin with goat's hair to resemble his hairy brother. Once prepared, she sent Jacob in bearing a meal for Isaac, resulting in Jacob receiving the blessing intended for Esau.

Upon hearing the news, Esau was livid. He exclaimed, "Isn't Jacob just living up to his name? He's cheated me twice now – first my birthright, and now my blessing!" This deception ignited a violent rage in Esau, who vowed to take Jacob's life once their father passed away.

With his mother's urging, Jacob left for Haran to reside with Uncle Laban, escaping Esau's fury. Once again, Rebekah conned

Isaac, claiming that she was heartbroken by Jacob wanting to marry a Canaanite bride from Heth's lineage. Convinced, Isaac consented to send Jacob away to find a suitable wife among Rebekah's relatives.

On his journey to Haran, Jacob paused for a break in Bethel, where he experienced a vivid dream. In his vision, a ladder connected Earth to the heavenly gates, with angels ascending and descending between the two realms. This powerful dream gave Jacob deep spiritual insight and a sense of wonder.

CHAPTER 4

THE CLASH OF CIVILIZATIONS

"Jacob's Journey of Deception and Triumph"

In Haran, Jacob fell in love with the younger daughter of Laban, but on the night of the wedding, Laban covered his older daughter Leah's face with a veil as the bride. In a tale of cunning and deception, Jacob worked diligently for seven long years, tending to his uncle Laban's flock, all for the love of Laban's beautiful daughter, Rachel. Much to Jacob's dismay, Laban tricked him by insisting that Leah, the younger sister, should be married off first. Despite this betrayal, Laban promised to also give Rachel as a wife to Jacob in exchange for another seven years of labor. A week later, the marriage between Rachel and Jacob was finally successful. As a result, with Jacob's blessings upon him, Laban experienced tremendous prosperity.

After 14 long years of service, Jacob decided it was time to return to his homeland, taking his family with him. Laban, however, had a problem – he felt like there was some unpaid debt between them. With the Lord's blessings, Jacob's expert care for Laban's livestock had led to a substantial increase in their numbers. Worried about what was owed to him, Laban asked, "What can I give you?" Jacob confidently replied, "You don't need to give me a thing… Just let me walk through your flock today and take the speckled and spotted sheep and goats, as well as the brown lambs. If you find any among mine later, it'll mean they were stolen."

Laban craftily removed all the spotted and speckled creatures, handing them over to his sons, thinking he could halt the production of mixed-colored animals like goats, calves, camels, and donkeys. However, with divine assurance, Jacob's flocks astonishingly conceived numerous speckled and spotted offspring. This miraculous event continued for six years, dramatically increasing Jacob's flock. The remaining dull brown animals became Laban's property, sparking envy among Laban's sons towards Jacob.

Over six years, Jacob amassed a fortune through sheep, goats, and cattle, becoming a prosperous man with profound spiritual convictions. Two decades had gone by since the cunning encounter between Jacob and Esau.

As Jacob journeyed towards Canaan with his family, herders, and livestock, he sent messengers ahead to meet his brother. Fearing Esau's wrath, divine intervention came in the form of a celestial army of angels for Jacob's protection. Upon witnessing this divine assembly, Jacob named the location Mahanaim, signifying 'This is God's camp'.

Alone, after crossing the Jordan River, Jacob found himself in a captivating midnight encounter with an enigmatic angel. They wrestled tirelessly until the angel granted him a blessing. As daybreak approached, their battle ended with Jacob's hip dislocated.

In Genesis Chapter 32, Jacob ultimately revealed his name to the angel, which meant "liar, cheater, and schemer." The angel then proclaimed, "From now on, you shall be called Israel instead of Jacob; for you have triumphed in your battles with both God and men."

After two long decades, Jacob felt it was time to make amends with Esau. As their reunion drew near, Jacob thoughtfully sent a generous assortment of presents, hoping to win his brother's forgiveness and spare his life.

As dawn broke, Jacob was filled with fear when he learned that Esau was drawing near with 400 men. Swiftly, he divided his children among his wives and maidservants. To his astonishment, Esau warmly embraced him, refusing the extravagant gifts and making peace between them. Overcome by joy, Jacob bowed seven times before Esau and sobbed. He insisted on presenting abundant gifts and livestock to Esau, who humbly responded, "I have plenty, my brother; keep what you have for yourself" (Gen. 33:9).

At last, Esau accepted the gifts to make amends and invited Jacob to journey home together. The brothers went their separate ways after reuniting and only came back together to lay their father to rest at the age of 180 in the cave of Machpelah in Hebron. They both moved past their bitter history, choosing to live apart in peace.

Jacob settled in Shechem, a northern part of Canaan. There, he purchased some land from King Shechem's son, Hamor, and maintained his family's nomadic lifestyle amid the rugged landscape. Meanwhile, Esau's family ventured to a distant land, away from Jacob's influence. They established themselves at Mount Seir in the land of Edom. Both brothers flourished over time and amassed great wealth, making it impossible for them to coexist side by side.

Following the rape of Dinah, the daughter of Jacob and Leah, the family migrated to Bethel, another region of Canaan, for safety. Shechem first raped Dinah; then, his father pleaded to Jacob for her hand in marriage to his son. Jacob's sons deceived the men by persuading them to circumcise every male; then, they promised to give Dinah in marriage and become one people. The men agreed to be circumcised.

Then on the third day, when the men were in pain, Simeon and Levi killed Hamor and Shechem with the sword and captured Dinah. Jacob's sons went into the city of Shechem, killed all the men, and looted the town. Jacob rebuked his sons for the terrible ordeal, saying: "You have troubled me by making me obnoxious among the land's inhabitants, the Canaanites and the Perizzites," he said. Jacob took all foreign idols away from his sons and built an altar in Bethel to God. Later, Jacob and his family moved to the valley of Hebron to settle.

The Philistines, Pagans, and the Rise of Christianity

In the early chapters of the Bible, we meet intriguing seafaring people such as the Philistines, Casluhim, Caphtorim, and Pathrusim. They arrived from a distant land across the ocean. As a child, Abraham listened astonished to tales of these fierce marauders plundering Hamite territories along the Mediterranean coast.

The Caphtorim and Pathrusim, also called the Hyksos in Egypt, wreaked havoc on the island of Crete before moving on to Mesopotamia. Their terror-filled campaign in Crete involved ravaging farmland and torching cities. Once they conquered this new territory, the Aryans moved in and set up Greco-Roman colonies ruled by powerful monarchs.

In the New Testament, Paul received inspiration from Titus to fortify the church in Crete by teaching solid doctrine. Interestingly, Paul cited a seventh-century poet, Epimenides of Knossos, who possessed prophetic abilities and famously declared, "Cretans are always liars, evil beasts, lazy gluttons... 'They claim to know God, but their actions betray them, being disobedient and unworthy of any good deed.'"

Since Greeks were known for their captivating storytelling, Paul cleverly referenced a popular tale about a renowned philosopher who had been captured and resisted foretelling positive outcomes for the Greco-Aryans living in Crete. Holding Indo-European roots himself, Titus felt that the Greeks had strayed as faith educators by twisting Christianity into a means of acquiring earthly wealth and upholding their pagan beliefs.

Paul cautioned the gentiles not to fall for the flawed beliefs of ancient Greek gods by involving themselves in demonic rituals. In Greco-Crete, Dionysus's mysterious ceremonies, which linked to Bacchus and Liberalia festivals, connected trance-inducing plants and the intoxicating effects of wine with unveiling cosmic secrets. These festivities were tied to fertility practices, and followers believed that gods roamed the Earth in human form.

Upon reaching Athens, the heart and philosophical hub of ancient Greece, Paul witnessed a city full of public celebrations dedicated to numerous deities. Pagan temples were prominently visible atop Greece's sacred hills. One remarkable example was the Temple of Artemis at Ephesus an architectural marvel surpassing even the renowned Parthenon. This magnificent structure, wholly constructed from marble, stood as a tribute to the Greek's pagan deity.

Paul journeyed to the bustling marketplace, the Agora, enthusiastically sharing Jesus Christ's resurrection story. Word spread about Paul's miraculous healing of a man who had never walked before in Lystra. Astonished, the crowd hailed him as a god, exclaiming, "The gods have descended to us as humans!"

As Paul amassed followers, he boldly denounced superstitious beliefs without fear of offending. He felt compelled to address the gentiles in a letter to the Corinthian church, asserting that one cannot worship both God and idols. During his visit to Corinth, he observed how idolatry pervaded their religious practices.

Paul's refreshing message was all about loving God wholeheartedly and embracing universal love for humankind.

In his teachings, Christ had paid for humanity's sins – for both Jews and gentiles – marking a new beginning with the gospel or "good news." However, Paul cautioned gentiles not to misuse this newfound salvation by associating with demonic forces.

Paul possessed the remarkable ability to heal the sick and expel malevolent spirits from those who could predict the future. Along with his followers, he orchestrated a significant public incineration of magical texts and religious icons deemed pagan. This perplexing aspect of superstitious culture was entwined with daily life, meddling with the wealth of the elite class. For Paul, these arcane traditions were nothing short of blasphemous.

Apostle Paul faced opposition to his ground-breaking concept of uniting humanity under "The Way," encountering hostility from multiple fronts. Furious crowds of Jews accused him of desecrating their holy temple, while Roman authorities branded him a terrorist for stirring up trouble. Christians from Iconium and neighboring areas flocked to catch a glimpse of Paul before he set off for Spain.

Paul's conviction that salvation was available to all – regardless of background – symbolized divine approval for both Jews and Gentiles. However, imposing such beliefs on those who regarded the Hebrews as second-class citizens threatened to incite even more accusations of blasphemy by ordinary folk.

In the ancient city of Lystra, situated in the Roman province of Galatia, Paul faced a brutal attack. An enraged crowd dragged him out of town and left him for dead. The reason? Paul was associated with Jesus of Nazareth, a Palestinian Jew from Galilee—a hotbed for the infamous Jewish militant group known as the Zealots.

The Zealots were fierce opponents of Roman rule and passionate about freeing their homeland. They morphed into an extremist group, refusing any compromise with their pagan adversaries occupying their sacred lands. Engaged in a struggle for Palestine's independence, they allied with the Edomites and vowed to battle until death.

Miraculously, Paul was rescued by a group of Roman soldiers and taken to Antonia Fortress as a prisoner. He was later moved to Caesarea to stand trial.

Long before Paul's teachings of God's kingdom and Jesus Christ, the Aryan Hyksos invaded Mesopotamia, ruthlessly looting, killing, and incinerating villages in their path. They destroyed entire cities, murdering men and enslaving women and children. A coalition was formed by Joshua, uniting warriors from the Mediterranean Coast, including Jordanians, Lebanese, and Cushites to launch a surprise night attack on the Philistine kings. Non-Exodus Hebrews who hadn't gone to Egypt and numerous subjugated Cushites also fought against their mutual foes.

The local Canaanites, Jebusites, and Hittites, with ancestral ties to the prominent Hebrew clan, rallied behind the Israelites led by Joshua. Together with their allies, they waged war against the five Hyksos (Amorite) kings and pursued them on the road leading to Beth Horon.

In the highly fortified twin cities of Upper and Lower Beth Horon, the residents swiftly fled as far as Azekah and Makkedah. During their escape, the Lord showered massive hailstones upon them from the heavens. To ensure his people had ample time for retaliation against their enemies, the Lord ordered the sun to pause over Gibeon, while the moon remained motionless in the Valley of Aijalon (Josh. 10:10).

As for Esau, despite forgiving his brother Jacob, their descendants became entangled in never-ending conflicts, fueling generations of animosity. Both Esau and Jacob faced shared foes that transcended religious, political, and ethnic boundaries. Prophets sent by the Lord cautioned them about a northern group who would attempt to deceive them and strip away their rightful claim to their land.

Prophet Amos witnessed a breach in the brotherly covenant, and he knew God would enact punishment. Warning six neighboring nations, Amos spoke of their impending downfall due to their oppression of the poor and idol worship. He specifically detailed Moab's offense: the desecration of the King of Edom's remains by burning them to lime. Amos prophesied that a consuming fire would destroy Moab and its palaces. Contrary to creating unity, the prophets reprimanded both Ammonites and Edomites for taking pleasure in Israel and Judah's discomfiture.

The origins of the Ammonites and Moabites are traced back to Lot's incestuous relations with his daughters. Living in the mountains of Zoar, the daughters intoxicated their father with wine and led him to commit incest, believing there were no other virtuous men left on earth.

Following Esau's death, the Edomites capitalized on the Israelites' vulnerabilities, seeking vengeance for past disputes. Ethnic blending and strong northern influences only fueled the animosity between Isaac's sons.

Some scholars argue that the Indo-European involvement intensified the hatred, as Aryans often aligned themselves with the Arab or Moorish clans that eventually embraced Islam. It's fascinating to consider that the once dark-skinned region inhabited by both Edomites and Israelites changed dramatically due to the Aryan Hyksos migration.

The story of Joseph

As Joseph and his brothers cared for their father's sheep, he recounted vivid dreams that sparked both pride and jealousy among his siblings. His father had gifted him a unique, multicolored coat laden with a plethora of hues, symbolizing adoration; however, this gift ultimately became a source of envy within the family. Although Joseph held the title of the firstborn to Rachel, he ranked as Jacob's eleventh and most cherished son. Tragically, Rachel met her end en route to Ephrath (Bethlehem), during the birth of their second child, Benjamin.

Joseph was only seventeen at the time of his two dreams. He said, "Then behold, my sheaf arose and stood upright; and indeed, your sheaves stood all around and bowed down to my sheaf."

The Lord had given Joseph a prophetic vision of his family bowing down to him, which came true some thirteen years later. The dream brought jealousy into the heart of his brothers.

Joseph's brothers' hatred grew even stronger after he shared his second dream. Genesis 37:9 recounts the dream, "Look, I had another dream. This time, the sun, moon, and eleven stars bowed down to me." When Joseph narrated this dream to his father, he received a stern reprimand. "What kind of dream have you had? Are your mother, brothers, and I supposed to bow down to you?"

Not long after this divine vision, Jacob (Israel) sent his sons to tend their flock in Shechem while Joseph stayed behind. Later, Joseph was tasked with checking on his brothers and their sheep. This fueled even more resentment among the siblings, leading them to plot Joseph's murder. When Joseph couldn't find his brothers in the pasture, he asked a helpful stranger for their location. The stranger informed him that they had mentioned going to a town called Dothan.

As Joseph approached from afar, one sibling jeered, "Here comes the dreamer! Let's kill him, throw him into a pit, and claim a wild beast devoured him. We'll see about his dreams then!" However, Reuben, the eldest brother, intervened, "Don't kill him... Don't spill any blood. Put him in this wilderness pit and don't touch him." Reuben secretly hoped to save Joseph and rescue him later.

As Joseph approached his siblings, they forcefully removed his coat and threw him into an empty, dry cistern nearby. While they were having a meal, a caravan of Ishmaelite merchants passed by, their camels laden with spices, balm, and myrrh on their journey to Egypt. Judah then made an urgent appeal to his brothers: "Why should we murder our own brother and hide his blood? Instead, let's sell him to these Ishmaelites – that way we won't harm him directly since he is, after all, our own flesh and blood."

Agreeing with the plan, the brothers hoisted Joseph out of the cistern and sold him to the traders for twenty silver coins. In Egypt, Joseph was ultimately sold to Potiphar, a high-ranking official in Pharaoh's court. Unaware of his son's true fate for the next two decades, Jacob mourned Joseph relentlessly, believing he was dead.

A sense of mysticism lingers over the Israelites, Edomites, and all of Arabia, a region that continues to impact global peace. The entangled history of these groups, often manipulated for the benefit of outsiders, presents a significant barrier. Esau is one figure whose negative influence seems to have pervaded the region extensively. However, is it possible that the Middle East's troubled fate has been portrayed through the eyes of an aggressor aiming to vilify Esau for their own interests?

In today's world, the discord in the Middle East stems less from the ancient rivalry between Jacob and Esau and more from the actions of greedy European colonizers who exploited the region for personal gain. At first glance, it might appear that the Middle East and Africa are plagued by age-old conflicts and strife. But in reality, internal battles and religious intolerance have caused an isolation of governments and people from the rest of the world.

Delving into the various eras of European dominance, we uncover striking resemblances in their psychological and spiritual beliefs, which many religious leaders label as a necessary evil. Early Indo-Europeans were convinced that dismantling civilizations would subject people to their will, gaining favor from numerous pagan deities. Similarly, Christian conquerors in the New World considered it essential to transform their savage nobility to good by granting absolute authority to white European colonizers.

This thought process, deeply ingrained in European culture, bears intriguing parallels with the historical dynamics witnessed in the early history of Israel. Just as Europeans claimed to act in service of God while ruthlessly forcing their victims into submission, the Hebrews too found themselves entangled in a complex web of alliances, betrayals, and cultural assimilation.

Within European culture, the legacy of brutality, famine, torture, and greed created a tragic narrative that resonates even today, giving birth to the enigmatic Babylon. Similarly, in ancient Israel, the early judges and kings sought the aid of remnants from the Edomite lineage to confront their mutual adversaries. However, this reliance on bloodline connections proved to be a double-edged sword.

The Edomites, Moabites, and Ammonites, all sharing blood ties, sometimes became a troublesome presence for the nation of Israel. As described by the authors of the Bible, the Hebrews began adopting pagan customs mirroring those of the foreign settlers in the land of Ham. Gradually, this led to a transformation of the Hebrews into adversaries of Israel, a development that mirrored the European cultural assimilation and the subsequent emergence of a ruthless mindset in service of God.

Thus, the intertwining narratives of European culture and ancient Israel showcase the profound impact of shared histories of brutality, cultural assimilation, and the paradoxical claim of acting in service of a higher power. These echoes reverberate through time, shaping the tragic legacies and enigmatic aspects of both cultures.

Then he sent to Jehoshaphat, King of Judah, saying, "The King of Moab has rebelled against me. Will you go with me to fight against Moab?" And he said, "I will go up; I am as you are my people as your people, my horses as your horses...So the king of Israel went with the king of Judah and the king of Edom, and they marched on that roundabout route seven days"
(2 Kings 3:7–9).

CHAPTER 5

THE IMPERIALIST POWERS

In the early chapters of the Bible, a powerful Indo-European force known as the Five Kings, or the Tidal of Nations, surged through the Afro-Asiatic and Cushite lands now recognized as Africa and the Middle East. This powerful wave redefined geographical boundaries without considering local cultures and established a social hierarchy based on class and privilege. These foreign conquerors spread across the globe, building empires in their quest for global dominance that continues to this day.

Fast forward to the 19th century, European imperial powers prolonged their reach over Africa's riches. It wasn't long before their insatiable appetite extended to the Middle East, stirring up unrest in the region. England, France, and Germany grew their political influences using diplomacy, igniting tensions in Middle Eastern territories. Meanwhile, Belgium, Dutch, France, Great Britain, Germany, Italy, Portugal, Russia, and Spain exploited vulnerable nations by applying political or military pressure to make them submit to their rule. The welfare of the people in these conquered regions mattered little to these ravenous nations.

The African plains and the Middle East, home to the Afro-Asiatic people, have contributed immensely to the cultural heritage of the early biblical era. Various tribes of the Hamitic people made their homes in eastern Arabia, stretching from Havilah to Shur, just east of Egypt, where once upon a time, the Garden of Eden was encircled by four rivers. The Hamites also established themselves in different parts of Africa and the Middle East before a new conquering power took over the area.

During the late 19th century, Britain, France, and Italy were in fierce competition to secure the Suez Canal, a key strategic location for maintaining access to vital trade routes towards India. This sparked a race among Europe's major powers to seize Africa's wealth of resources, particularly along the banks of the Nile River. Driven by their ambitions, these nations vied for territorial expansion and control over trade in this enigmatic land. Portugal and France had already established a presence on Africa's west coast – in Ghana and Angola – as well as on Mozambique's eastern shores.

In a fierce battle for supremacy, the Dutch and British vied for the gold and diamond-laden lands of South Africa. The escapades of intrepid explorers and missionaries in Africa captured headlines, as European newspapers eagerly chronicled their every move.

The explorers returned with tales of vast, lush jungles, towering mountains capped with snow, and a diversity of wildlife unseen by Europeans. Their stories ignited widespread fascination for the African continent. People imagined Africa teeming with unimaginable wealth, from bountiful river basins to hidden troves of gold, diamonds, silver, ivory, coal, and copper.

In 1876, King Leopold II of Belgium initiated a brutal campaign to conquer Central Africa, destroying villages to establish settlements in the Congo. Conflicts arose among Britain, France, and Belgium over control of this prized territory. However, Leopold cunningly declared himself emperor of the Congo Free State and allowed open trade for all European nations.

To deceive the public and build his empire in Central Africa, Leopold established the International Association for Exploration and Civilization of Congo under the guise of humanitarian and missionary work.

Numerous Africans were forcibly taken from the Congo and sold in the European slave trade. Leopold established Boma as the capital on the Congo River's north bank, dividing the Congo Free State into 14 administrative regions. For over two decades, he implemented a brutal forced labor system to extract rubber, ivory, and food, resulting in a massive population decline due to illness and starvation.

Leopold also abducted African children, raising them to serve in his Force Publique army, enforcing his oppressive slave labor laws. The horrifying corruption was so severe that it drew public condemnation from many European visitors who witnessed the heinous crimes.

In 1891, Leopold proclaimed that the Congo's natural resources were now the property of the Congo Free State. The locals would be compensated by government officials for gathering these valuable assets. Soon, agents were stationed in each village, supported by a police force to oversee the natives' labor and trade activities.

The Free State agents collaborated with village chiefs to allot food and resources to privately-owned businesses acting as state representatives. These agents were well-equipped, and even young children were subjected to harsh labor conditions or faced punishment by a rugged hippopotamus-hide whip.

Leopold established an extensive transportation network of roads and railways, connecting the abundant raw materials from Congo's interior to coastal ports for shipment to Belgium. Vast quantities of rubber, ivory, and other materials from the upper Congo basin found their way to factories worldwide. Merciless beatings or death penalties awaited those who failed to meet minimal rubber collection quotas. When such quotas were not met, militants had no choice but to present severed hands of Congolese victims as justification for falling short.

The merciless massacre of countless innocents paved the way for the plundering of Congo's rich natural resources, ultimately transforming Brussels into the majestic capital of Belgium. Leopold didn't stop there - he brought African wildlife to populate Belgian zoos.

To maintain control, he established a formidable military force, constructing 183 forts throughout the Congo and enforcing his extreme labor laws. The Force Publique army was responsible for rounding up workers in the most horrifying manner. When people fought back, the soldiers unleashed unspeakable acts of brutality.

In numerous instances, these soldiers returned bearing baskets filled with severed heads, hands, and unmentionable body parts belonging to their victims. Women and children were decapitated, their lifeless bodies gruesomely displayed on poles in the shape of a cross - a terrifying symbol of retribution for defiance against his rule.

The grueling sight of human heads and various body parts mounted on enormous skull racks awaited their fate at the hands of the Force Publique army. Prisoners, in dismay, found themselves shackled and ordered to trudge deep into the forests, only after witnessing their villages being set on fire by the Force Publique army. Their purpose: to extract rubber plant sap for the ever-growing appetite of Europe.

Farmland was completely flattened to welcome the burgeoning rubber industry that supplied European markets. Meanwhile, Belgian overlords seized Congolese farmers from their homeland to cultivate Africa's valuable agricultural goods on Belgium's soil.

The blood money generated from Congo's forced labor enabled Leopold to fund grandiose constructions such as royal palaces, glasshouses, coastal resorts, public works projects, free schools, museums and sculptural monuments – all in honor of Belgium's royalty.

The horrifying events in the Congo gained widespread attention during the early 1900s, turning into a massive global controversy. In this dark period, the brutal treatment inflicted upon the native Congolese led to a staggering death toll ranging between 10 and 15 million.

Egypt found itself financially constrained amid the clashing political forces of Great Britain and France, both vying for Anglo-Saxon supremacy. As a result, Europeans dominated Egypt's commercial landscape, relegating Egyptians to second-class status. While the locals bore a hefty tax burden, their European counterparts enjoyed increasing wealth. European powers reshaped Egypt's governance through imperialist policies, reinforcing a belief in white Anglo-Saxon superiority.

In the summer of 1881, tensions grew over unjust discrimination, leading to Egyptian officers taking control and forming a new government. In June 1882, violent riots erupted in Alexandria, targeting businesses throughout Egypt. The British and French struck back with a powerful naval force in Alexandria, bombarding the city. They then sent 25,000 soldiers to Ismailia, causing Egypt to surrender.

Meanwhile, as European powers expanded their reach across Africa and the Middle East, the United States extended its territory towards the Pacific Ocean. Mexico was pressured into giving up the northern third of its land for a mere $15 million to the US, allowing America's border expansion to continue. Just five years after the Spanish-American War, the United States obtained the beautiful South Pacific islands of Hawaii, transforming it into a crucial military base. The year was 1893 and ambitious American businessmen, backed by US Marines, launched a revolution to overthrow Queen Liliuokalani and dismantle the Hawaiian monarchy. This turned Hawaii into the nation's fiftieth state.

Taking a step back in time, an age-old belief held that the mighty Anglo-Saxon civilization had a divine authority to govern the world and subjugate lesser societies. This ideology had its roots deep within the landscapes of Europe. A particular concept claimed that the superior Anglo-Saxon meant that they were naturally selected to thrive, while the suppressed remained powerless — essentially validating a massive campaign of genocide according to Charles Darwin's theory. These concepts became popularly known as the survival of the fittest and the origin of species, which laid the groundwork for Darwin's revolutionary ideas.

These ambitious individuals weren't shy about expressing their global aspirations. Their primary interest was in securing untold wealth worldwide through ruthless campaigns. The ultimate aim was to seize entire vast geographical areas and tap into their plentiful resources for personal gain.

Throughout history, countless civilizations have been targeted due to race, ethnicity, or religion. Often, the most vulnerable members of these societies, such as women and children, suffered the most when aggressors tried to seize power from existing governments. At the core of this issue were the European superpowers striving to establish their imperial control over these newfound territories for self-serving purposes.

In 1909, a fresh political group called the Young Turks emerged in the Ottoman Empire after a fierce civil war. This conflict involved Abdul Hamid II employing Kurds and Turkish peasants to launch brutal attacks on Armenian villages, resulting in the deaths of hundreds of thousands of Armenians.

When World War I erupted in August 1914, many Armenians joined forces with Russia and separated from the new Turkish government. In response, the Ottoman Empire's new leadership sided with Germany and the Central Powers against Great Britain, France, and Russia to reclaim lost territories from the Russo-Turkish war of 1877-1878.

In a covert operation, the new Turkish government targeted and captured prominent Armenian figures such as politicians, religious leaders, writers, and educators, executing them without delay. They indiscriminately rampaged from one village to another, burning houses and businesses. Many who tried to flee were chained together and thrown into rivers to drown.

Armenian soldiers who had joined the Turkish forces were disarmed and dispatched to labor camps, where they faced execution. Whole communities were terrorized, with women and children stripped naked and paraded out of their villages. Ultimately, the remaining Armenians were forcibly deported to the harsh deserts and swamps of Syria, left to die from thirst and starvation. It is estimated that close to a million Armenians perished during this horrifying genocide.

On August 4, 1914, Germany marched through Belgium territory to invade France after Archduke Francis Ferdinand, heir to the throne of the Austro-Hungarian Empire, and his wife, Duchess Sophia, were assassinated in Sarajevo, Bosnia. The couple was killed on June 28, 1914, by a Serbian terrorist group, the Black Hand, dedicated to creating a Pan-Slavic kingdom.

On July 29, the Soviet Union sprang into action, deploying its forces to defend Serbia from an impending Austrian/German invasion. Then, on August 4, Great Britain valiantly entered the fray against Germany, standing up for Belgium's sovereignty after the Germans turned down a plea to vacate neutral Belgium by midnight on August 3.

Despite American President Woodrow Wilson's declaration of neutrality, he had a soft spot for the Allies during World War I and passionately urged all sides to reach a peace agreement. Taking advantage of the ongoing conflict, the United States sold supplies to both the Allies and Central Powers, fostering a thriving war economy in the process.

Meanwhile, the Allies flexed their naval muscles with the powerful British fleet imposing a suffocating blockade on European ports. In response, Germany unleashed its deadly U-boats—submarines that wreaked havoc on commercial and passenger ships en route to Allied ports from the United States, sinking tons upon tons of crucial supplies.

During the war's initial phase, the Russians captured approximately 130,000 prisoners and inflicted over 300,000 casualties in the fierce Battle of Galicia. A multitude of Slavic soldiers surrendered, with some even volunteering to join the Russian ranks. The Italians shifted their allegiance, abandoning the Central Powers for the Allies. This move greatly assisted Russia in securing nearly all of Galicia by 1914's close.

However, the tide shifted to defeat when the Central Powers focused on the pivotal Battle of Tannenberg in winter. They launched an assault on the Russians in Galicia's southern region along the Eastern Front. Consequently, the Russians retreated about three hundred miles eastward toward Warsaw's vicinity. The situation worsened as Bulgaria declared war on Serbia in September 1915, aligning with the Central Powers. This deadly blow crushed both Serbia and Romania while allowing Germany access to crucial supplies via this newfound alliance.

During a time when social Darwinism and racism were at their peak, Europeans challenged the natural boundaries of humanity, exploiting resources to serve Anglo-Saxon interests. The belief in Darwin's theory suggested that a dominant race must assert its power over weaker ones to display the might and vigor of the superior society.

Numerous Africans became pawns in this power struggle, forced to fight for European-controlled colonies and deepening divisions within their own lands. Meanwhile, Europe was gearing up for total war, extending its influence across most of Africa and consequently dragging the continent onto European battlegrounds.

As 1917 drew to a close, the United States joined the fray in the third year of a brutal war, serving as reinforcements in several key Allied battles. The root of the conflict lay in the insatiable hunger for territories driven by imperialist competition. Despite this, African-Americans chose to fight with the goal of advancing democracy around the world, hoping to stake their claim in the lofty Western ideals of liberty and equality.

Both Africans and African-Americans actively and passively participated in the conflict, giving rise to a new generation of young individuals prepared to battle for their newfound dreams of national pride. Countless people who lived under colonial rule shared this newfound faith in democracy as a means to ensure global safety; they fought fiercely on European and African soil alike. Though oppression was rife worldwide, many remained hopeful that these revolutionary ideas of freedom could bring about change.

On February 23, 1917, Russia made an abrupt exit from the war due to a revolution that toppled Czar Nicholas II from power. However, fresh Armenian forces soon took their place on the side of the Allies. The captivating appeal of cultural identity and independence outshone, and even the intensity of class conflicts took a secondary role in fueling the fervor of ideological passion. Finally, as November 9, 1918 saw Allied forces intensify their efforts against Germany, Kaiser Wilhelm was forced into exile in Holland. The war came to an end just two days later.

In an effort to establish lasting peace and prevent future conflicts, President Wilson proposed the Fourteen Points plan following the devastating World War I, which claimed the lives of around nine million soldiers and left over twenty-two million wounded. The war's impact extended far beyond the battlefield; it's estimated that civilian casualties doubled due to starvation and a plummeting birthrate.

The significant Treaty of Sèvres was signed on August 10, 1920, granting England and France control over valuable oil-rich Ottoman territories in Asia and Africa. Great Britain received authority over Israel, the West Bank, and Jordan, while the area between the Jordan River and Mediterranean Sea became known as Palestine - thus separating it from Israel.

For centuries, people from diverse religious backgrounds coexisted harmoniously, but that harmony was about to shatter. Western powers drew new borders to serve their own motives, driving a wedge between once-peaceful neighbors. This ignited tensions as the ruling authorities shifted their loyalty towards foreign influences, neglecting the needs and interests of their citizens.

CHAPTER 6

A DEVASTATING IMPACT ON EUROPEAN AND AFRICAN ECONOMIES AND COMMUNITIES

World War I crippled the European economic system and slowed the progress of the United States' financial market due to overproduction once the war ended. As the war concluded, Great Britain reeled from both economic and emotional wounds, mourning the loss of a million soldiers. In the United States, the farming and mining sectors faced an overwhelming surplus of goods, causing profits to plummet.

The Roaring Twenties were riddled with hardships for African American communities, as a shocking 80% of them lived as tenants on farms. The situation was dire, with one in four repossessed farms being sold at auctions due to unpaid mortgage loans. The atmosphere was tense in the South, as white men expressed their rage and frustration by reviving the heinous act of lynching against African Americans.

A significant number of African Americans found themselves jobless as white workers snatched away their employment opportunities. As the Great Depression intensified, families across racial lines struggled to make ends meet, turning to charity for survival. Meanwhile, young people wandered from one town to another in search of work and a better life.

In urban areas, many landlords decided not to rent to black families. Other landowners raised the rent, making it more difficult for blacks to budget their income, so African American families had to live together in tightly congested buildings.

Germany and Italy went on a campaign of terror when the two countries embraced an idea of Aryan racial purity, believing that white Anglo-Saxons were the master race considering people of African blood to be savage and subhuman.

Germany teetered on the edge of civil war as starvation gripped the nation after World War I. The consequences of the conflict rippled throughout other Anglo-Saxon countries, igniting political, cultural, and social shifts across Europe, Asia, and Africa. At the turn of the 20th century, Germany embarked on a quest in Namibia to seize land and livestock from two tribal groups in South-West Africa. The native Namibians' territory was handed over to white settlers, transforming it into German South-West Africa.

The indigenous inhabitants of South-West Africa found themselves restricted to reservation camps until a rebellion against colonial rule broke out, which continued for three years. In response, the Germans ruthlessly pursued a campaign to wipe out those indigenous Namibians who defied their colonization efforts.

They then strategically encircled the city but left a desert escape route for locals. As violence forced the Namibians to take refuge in the desert, they were barred from returning. This cruel tactic exposed them to extreme hunger and dehydration–a plight made worse by suspicions that German forces had poisoned desert water wells.

An estimated 60,000 to 100,000 indigenous individuals in South-West Africa faced unspeakable cruelty at the hands of German forces. With limited options, survivors chose surrender over opposition. Disobedience from any Namibian—women and children included—resulted in either execution or violent banishment.

To conduct experiments, Germans set up concentration camps where Namibians were enslaved and subjected to forced labor for German officials or colonists. A considerable number of South-West African women were subjected to sterilization on German authority orders.

Born in Braunau am Inn, Austria, Adolf Hitler was captivated by the myth of a superior Aryan race with blonde hair and blue eyes, as portrayed in the works of Richard Wagner, a renowned but controversial nineteenth-century poet known for his contributions to musical drama and anti-Semitic literature.

After four years in the military, Hitler moved to Germany in 1912 and embarked upon a political career that led him to become the nation's ultimate political and military leader. Once in power, Hitler announced a plan in July 1933 aimed at eradicating Romani people across Europe, as they were believed to have intermingled with the Negroid population and threatened the purity of the Aryan race.

The Romani people were often seen as social pariahs. New policies compelled them to register with authorities and restricted their travel, as well as barring them from marrying anyone of Aryan descent. The government started arresting the Roma, including women and children from mixed-race marriages, sending them to concentration camps for genetic research.

In October 1935, Italy, under dictator Benito Mussolini's iron fist, waged a devastating invasion against Ethiopia in the Horn of Africa. Utilizing machine guns, heavy artillery, tanks, and mustard gas dispensed from warplanes by the Italian Royal Air Force, they struck ruthlessly. Ethiopia's Emperor Haile Selassie pleaded with the League of Nations for support. However, following fruitless negotiations with Rome, the British pulled their navy out of the Mediterranean, allowing Italy to amass military resources along the coast.

In a daring Hannibal-style maneuver, the Ethiopians launched an attack on Eritrea, the Italian stronghold housing around forty thousand troops. Striking at the heart of Italy's defenses, they forced the Italians to retreat. The Ethiopian army then skillfully encircled them, causing over three thousand Italian casualties.

Unfortunately, the triumphant Ethiopians' success was short-lived. Italy escalated their chemical warfare tactics, crippling Haile Selassie's forces. As a result, over the next five years, Ethiopia was absorbed into Italy's East Africa Empire alongside Eritrea, Libya, and Somalia. The Italians even tried to coerce the Ethiopians into renouncing their ancient African Christian faith that dates back to the first millennium.

Before European influence introduced its own version of Christianity, Africa experienced and interpreted the religion through a unique perspective. Storied battles between Italy and Ethiopia have left a bitter taste in Italy's mouth, a grudge that stretches back centuries. A more recent conflict unfolded in November 1934 when Italian forces trespassed into Ethiopian territory by extending Somalia's borders and establishing a fort in the oasis town of Walwal without Ethiopian consent.

A particularly stinging defeat for the Italians happened during the colonization efforts in March 1896. At the Battle of Adwa, Menelik II commanded nearly 100,000 troops and successfully crushed the Italian army, resulting in the loss of almost 2,000 Italian lives.

In 1936, a powerful alliance was forged between Mussolini and Hitler, known as the Rome-Berlin Axis, with the aim of reclaiming lost territory from World War I. Surprisingly, Hitler faced minimal opposition when occupying Austria, Czechoslovakia, and the port of Memel. Austrians believed that joining Germany would bring them independence and overwhelmingly voted in favor of Hitler's invasion.

Concurrently, Germany pursued their policy of racial purity by targeting blacks residing in towns and cities along the Rhine River in Central Europe. The Treaty of Versailles had declared the Rhineland a demilitarized zone after World War I, but German inhabitants warmly welcomed their forces with jubilant cheers.

In a dramatic turn of events, the lives of African and mixed-race individuals in the Rhineland and Austria were drastically altered. During France's occupation, African soldiers from their colonies were stationed in German towns and cities, following the Axis defeat in World War I. Seeing an opportunity, German soldiers struck back and arrested those they deemed enemies of the Nazi regime, with Africans becoming their main targets. Consequently, many black individuals faced assassination or imprisonment by the Nazis.

Countless prisoners of war endured starvation, sterilization, or were subjected to medical experiments. Some were even worked to death in labor camps. Meanwhile, Germany assumed direct control of the Rhineland's government and political climate and annexed it with Austria – all without opposition from Great Britain or France.

Following World War, I, the United States and Great Britain faced economic depression, while Japan emerged as a dominant powerhouse in East Asia. Much like Germany, the Japanese considered themselves a superior race with divine entitlement to govern the Pacific and East Asia. Their primary goal was territorial expansion, driven by their desire for essential natural resources. This ambition spurred them to attack regions such as French-controlled Indochina (Cambodia, Laos, and Vietnam) in Southeast Asia and the Dutch-controlled East Indies.

From July to December 1937, the Chinese forces, caught off guard, suffered devastating losses as Japan bombarded major cities like Peking, Shanghai, and Nanking. The assault resulted in thousands of civilian casualties. Nanking alone witnessed an estimated 250,000 to 300,000 deaths, accompanied by rampant looting and sexual violence. By February 1939, Japan had conquered the majority of Eastern China along with the Hainan and Spratly Islands.

On September 1, 1939, the relentless German forces invaded Poland, marking the beginning of the Second World War. This once peaceful European country soon transformed into a chaotic battleground. Just days before, on August 23, Germany and Russia had secretly signed the chilling Nazi-Soviet Nonaggression Pact.

This unexpected partnership between the two nations set the stage for their joint invasion of Poland, splitting the land amongst themselves. Germany employed its fearsome blitzkrieg strategy - a ruthless mix of aerial bombardments followed by waves of tanks, artillery, and ground troops - overwhelming Poland's armed forces and forever altering the course of history.

Under the command of Joseph Stalin, the Russian forces launched a surprise attack from the east, cornering the unprepared Polish army. They justified their actions by claiming Poland's territory belonged to Russia. On September 17, 1939, following the German bombardment, Russia crossed into Poland to stake their claim on their portion of the land.

Once upon a time, Russia and Germany were bitter rivals. However, they shocked the world by joining forces in a nonaggression pact that paved the way for the Soviet Union to take control of Estonia, Latvia, and Lithuania.

As tanks and artillery paraded through the bustling streets, the Russians secretly schemed to gain control over political leaders, doctors, lawyers, writers, and Polish police officers. Joseph Stalin commanded the executions of tens of thousands of people in this chilling episode of history. Moreover, Nazis targeted Poland for its large population of Jewish community, whom they believed were inferior to their so-called "pure Aryan race."

The Nazi regime firmly believed that Jews, thought to have mixed African heritage, were inferior compared to the pure Anglo-Saxon race. They saw this as a danger to the German population's survival. As a result, numerous Jews faced exile, and those suspected of Jewish lineage were forced into concentration camps. Whole villages suffered devastation due to their ethnicity, religious beliefs, or resistance against the Nazis.

On September 3, 1939, Great Britain and France declared war on Germany, attempting to halt its conquest through a naval blockade during the Battle of the Atlantic. Anticipating a potential preemptive strike by Nazi forces in their quest for European domination, Great Britain enacted its first peacetime draft in July 1939.

On June 10th, 1940, Italy joined forces with Germany in the war to counter the Allied naval blockade. The German navy ramped up their U-boat attacks in the Atlantic, sinking numerous merchant ships and jeopardizing crucial Allied supplies. In May 1940, the lightning-fast German military had occupied the Netherlands, Norway, Denmark, Belgium, and Luxembourg. This strategic move put the Axis forces right at France's doorstep, setting the stage for Hitler's future maneuvers.

In a strategic move, the Italian Navy and Air Force targeted the North African island of Malta, home to Great Britain's primary Mediterranean Fleet base. Since 1835, the British had possessed the island, utilizing it as a crucial outpost for their air and naval forces to assault the Axis's vital shipping resources. The Germans and Italians launched a rigorous aerial onslaught, involving over three thousand bombing raids from June 11, 1940, aimed at subduing Malta's thriving populace.

The British strategically split their fleet between Alexandria and Gibraltar in North Africa while facing constant bombardment from German and Italian air defenses. By summer 1942, Malta finally capitulated to the Axis forces, transforming into a strategic hub for controlling shipping routes and airfields throughout the Mediterranean.

In the early days of May 1940, the low-lying countries of France, the Netherlands, Belgium, and Luxembourg found themselves succumbing to the relentless advance of Axis forces. In a daring move, the British government launched Operation Dynamo to evacuate British and French soldiers from Dunkirk, France. A fleet of large ships and small merchant boats raced to the beach, heroically rescuing over three hundred thousand Allied troops under relentless attack from German and Italian forces.

The British and French forces found themselves trapped, vulnerable targets for the rapidly advancing German military on the beaches near Dunkirk. It all started on May 13, when the Germans secured a critical position by capturing the Meuse Bridge at Sedan, eventually leading to the occupation of France. France's humiliation culminated on June 22, 1940, when they signed an armistice in the very same railroad car where Germany had surrendered in World War I.

Fast forward to June 1941, and Germany turned against its former ally – Russia – launching a surprise attack with a colossal army. Dubbed Operation Barbarossa, Hitler sent nearly four million troops on an unprecedented offensive against the Soviet Union through the Baltic States and Ukraine. This early morning invasion became known as history's most significant assault.

The Nazis unleashed their fearsome death squad, the *'Einsatzgruppen,'* in an attempt to annihilate densely populated Jewish and Gypsy communities in Russia, Poland, and Ukraine. They blamed these groups for Germany's defeat in World War I. Gypsies were thought to have descended from Indo-Europeans who had mixed with the dark-skinned inhabitants of India, giving them their distinctive appearance.

The Nazis harbored intense animosity towards the Jewish community, partly due to their belief that Jews secretly possessed African blood in their DNA. Upon conquering new territories, they assigned Einsatzgruppen units to round up political figures and Jews, taking them to isolated locations. Victims were herded into craters or valleys and brutally executed with machine gun fire. Shockingly, the murderers also dumped truckloads of lime on men, women, and children.

In response to Germany's grip on Europe, numerous European Jews attempted to renounce their ancestry. After capturing France, Hitler devised a plan to exile four million Jews to the island of Madagascar, located off southeast Africa's coast. He believed that Great Britain would soon submit to German control and consequently postponed Operation Sea Lion. As the Nazis continued their rampage, they looted homes and businesses belonging to black people and Jews, even torching synagogues and entire communities.

The Nazi regime launched a ruthless campaign, targeting black people, Jews, and Gypsies to be imprisoned in concentration camps, where they were subjected to terrible experiments, deportation, or death by gassing or burning. As Germany claimed triumphs across Europe, the merciless Nazis orchestrated large-scale massacres in racially diverse communities. Numerous black Africans, unable to conceal their identities, were exploited as human guinea pigs and exposed to a variety of viruses such as hepatitis strains and other illnesses that eventually spread across Africa.

On September 27, 1940, the Axis alliance was forged as Germany, Japan, and Italy signed the Tripartite Pact. They vowed to back each other up in case any other country, like the United States, attacked them. Japan was on a mission to expand its empire and urgently needed resources like oil, fuel, and raw materials after the US cut off trade due to Japan's occupation of former French colonies in Indochina.

The increasing Japanese military presence in East Asia led the United States to freeze all Japanese assets within its borders. Great Britain joined the effort by imposing an embargo on Japan and demanding that it withdraw its troops from Indochina and China as well as exit the Tripartite Pact. With negotiations between Japan, Great Britain, and the United States collapsing, Japan secretly concocted a plan to strike at the US Pacific Fleet in Pearl Harbor, as well as British bases in the Philippines and Malaya – all with the aim of conquering land and resources essential for expanding its empire.

On the fateful morning of December 7, 1941, Commander Mitsuo Fuchida led a surprise attack by 183 Japanese high-altitude bombers and torpedo planes, accompanied by the formidable A6M3 Zero long-range fighters. Their primary targets were the aircraft carriers and battleships at the US naval base in Pearl Harbor, located on the beautiful island of Oahu, Hawaii.

The initial wave of bombers zeroed in on the colossal vessels at *Battleship Row*, while other assailants aimed for airfields and military bases. Ships like the *USS Oklahoma, Maryland, West Virginia, California,* and *Tennessee* were sitting ducks in the shallow harbor. Tragically, the *USS Oklahoma* and *West Virginia* suffered catastrophic damage from a simultaneous onslaught of high-level bombs and torpedoes.

Just past 8 AM, a devastating armor-piercing bomb struck the battleship *Arizona's* forward deck, igniting 500 tons of ammunition and claiming the lives of 1,177 sailors. The sheer force of the explosion ripped *Arizona* apart, sending the vessel to a watery grave in an instant. Less than an hour later, a second wave of 171 bombers targeted a major Pearl Harbor navy yard dry dock, landing a direct hit on the *Pennsylvania battleship*.

The *USS Cassin destroyer* wasn't spared either, as simultaneous attacks caused a fuel tank explosion, setting her ablaze and making her roll onto the nearby *USS Downes*. The situation worsened as ammunition aboard both ships detonated, causing severe damage. By the time the second wave subsided, a staggering 2,403 Americans and 59 Japanese had perished in this infamous assault.

On the very same day as the infamous Pearl Harbor attack, the Japanese air assault squadron shifted their focus toward the Philippines. Due to the International Date Line, this occurred on December 8, 1941. Their powerful aerial onslaught targeted Clark Field, just north of Manila, and Iba Airfield on Luzon's west coast. The catastrophic attack wiped out a significant portion of the heavy bombers and planes stationed there. As a result, the US Congress declared war on Japan that very day. This event signaled a turning point in the conflict as America abandoned its isolationist stance and unleashed its formidable military power to play a vital role in the fight.

On December 23, Japanese forces launched a relentless twelve-day assault on Wake Island, an American naval stronghold situated between Hawaii and the Mariana Islands. In the heat of the day, Japanese bombers from Kwajalein struck Wake Island, annihilating seven wildcat fighters stationed there. Miraculously, only one US aircraft on land and four in the sky were spared.

Caught off guard by an ill-prepared military, General Douglas MacArthur, leader of the Far East Air Force, found himself outmaneuvered as the Japanese seized air superiority. The situation grew even more perilous as Japanese ground forces invaded the Philippines, prompting General Douglas McArthur to make a daring escape to Australia.

By April 9, 1942, the Japanese forces captured the fortified island of Corregidor, and the Bataan Peninsula at the mouth of Manila Bay after a three-month battle. The following day, on

April 10, the Japanese forces rounded up thousands of prisoners to prepare for the infamous twelve-day Bataan Death March.

The prisoners faced the cruel reality of being denied basic necessities like food and water, before being forced to march towards Balanga, Bataan's capital, and Camp O'Donnell in San Fernando, situated in the Central Luzon region of the Philippines.

Numerous American and Filipino troops faced intentional starvation, and those who weakened from fatigue were either executed or mercilessly killed with bayonets and knives. The Japanese harbored deep resentment towards adversaries who fought fiercely, seeing prisoners of war as inferior beings undeserving of respect. The Philippine islands remained under Japanese control for another two and a half years. But then, on October 20, 1944, General Douglas McArthur made a triumphant return alongside the US Seventh Fleet during the three-day Battle of Leyte Gulf - the largest naval battle ever recorded in history.

On April 18, 1942, President Franklin D. Roosevelt ordered a thrilling air raid in response to the devastating Japanese attack on Pearl Harbor. This daring operation exposed Japan's susceptibility to US air assaults. Dubbed the Doolittle Raid, it marked the first-ever air strike on Japanese soil, launching sixteen B-25 Mitchell bombers from the USS *Hornet*—a new navy aircraft carrier sailing the western Pacific Ocean. The USS *Enterprise* and its fighters provided protection against possible Japanese assaults.

In the daring Doolittle Raid of 1942, a group of American bombers took off from an aircraft carrier and flew over Japan to strike back after the attack on Pearl Harbor. Most of the planes crash-landed or parachuted into China, where the brave citizens helped rescue the crew members, including the legendary Doolittle himself! However, not all of them were so lucky. Japanese forces captured eight crew members and executed three of them. Tragically, many Chinese citizens were also massacred for their heroic participation in saving American fighters.

But wait, there's more! One of the B-25 bombers managed to land safely in the Soviet Union at Vladivostok. However, instead of a warm welcome, the plane and its crew members were confiscated and detained for over a year by the Russians. Talk about a wild ride!

After the daring Doolittle Raid, President Franklin D. Roosevelt wanted to keep the Japanese guessing about where the bombers had come from. When asked, he slyly replied, "Shangri-La." Now, you might be wondering what on earth Shangri-La is! Well, it's an imaginary kingdom that many legendary explorers once believed was hidden in the Great Himalayas. It's said to be a utopia filled with Arabian Knights and other mystical wonders.

As winter set in, the German forces on the Eastern Front found themselves in a stalemate. They were trying to build up their military might, but the Soviets had other plans. They launched a strategic offensive that surrounded the Axis forces and led to a decisive victory for Russia! This was no small feat - it all went down in the Battle of Kursk, which was one of the largest tank encounters in history.

The Battle of Kursk was a turning point in World War II that set the stage for even more intense fighting to come. It was a moment that required bravery and skill from all those who fought in this pivotal conflict.

Following the battle, the new Russian aggression caused an uprising in the German-controlled eastern European countries. These countries immediately joined the Allied forces, adding even more strength to their cause. Meanwhile, Great Britain and American forces were invading French North Africa to ease pressure on the Soviet Union's fighting efforts. It was a complex and ever-changing war, but one thing was clear: everyone involved was willing to fight for what they believed in.

In June 1942, the German forces under the command of Erwin Rommel launched a brutal attack against the Allies in North Africa. With tanks and artillery, they recaptured eastern Benghazi, Libya, and by June 21st, they had taken the port of Tobruk. This was a huge victory for Rommel and the Afrika Korps, as they seized massive amounts of stored supplies.

But they weren't done yet! The German and Italian forces then crossed the border into Egypt through the Gazala Line, west of Tobruk. Their goal? To capture oil fields and supply lines across the desert. It was a bold move that would change the course of the war in North Africa.

By October of the Second El Alamein War, things were starting to look up for the Allied forces. The British took a defensive stance in Mersa Matruh on the Mediterranean coast to protect Alexandria. Meanwhile, Rommel's supplies were running low, and his troops were forced to use captured British vehicles to keep fighting against the Allies. Talk about a desperate situation!

But then, reinforcements arrived in the form of Italian foot soldiers, artillery units, and the 185th Airborne Division Folgore. It seemed like Rommel might just have a chance after all...or did he? The Allies weren't going down without a fight.

Battered by significant losses and with his Italian rear guard rapidly shrinking, Rommel realized that the moment had come for a strategic withdrawal from El Alamein. He prepared to head westward across the African desert toward Libya and Tunisia. It was a difficult decision, but one that he hoped would keep his troops alive and fighting for another day.

But the Allied forces weren't about to let him off that easy! Their victory at El Alamein marked the end of the Axis threat to the Suez Canal. Not only that, but it also gave the Allies easy access to the oil fields in the Middle East and Persian Gulf through North Africa. This became a game-changer!

By November 1942, Rommel had escaped from El Alamein and made his way to the Mareth Line. This was a crucial moment in the war, as both sides were gearing up for even more intense fighting.

The Allies had a bold plan to turn the tide of the war in North Africa. They would launch a covert mission to invade northwestern Africa's Moroccan, Algerian, and Tunisian territories, which were controlled by the Vichy French government. Their target? Key seaports and airfields that would allow them to attack the Axis forces rapidly through the eastern coast of Tunisia.

But that wasn't all! At the same time, the British Eighth Army would launch an assault from western Egypt, and would also send warships and submarines to Casablanca.

The objective of this massive invasion was clear: cut off the Axis from their supply lines and gain control of North Africa once and for all.

It was a bold move that would require precision planning and execution. But the Allies were ready to take on the challenge and fight for victory.

As the German Sixth Army crossed the Don River, Russia knew they had to act fast. They staged a defensive position in Stalingrad on the Eastern Front. But the Germans weren't going down without a fight. The Luftwaffe launched a five-day bombing campaign to control Caucasian oil fields and Stalingrad, an important industrial and administrative city of the Soviet Union.

In one of the first raids, hundreds of planes from the German Luftwaffe dropped incendiary bombs on Stalingrad. The result was catastrophic - a massive explosion that killed forty thousand civilians. It was a brutal attack that left many wondering what would happen next.

But the Battle of Stalingrad was far from over. The Russians were determined to defend their city and push back against the Axis forces

The combined casualty of Stalingrad is believed to be nearly two million people. Terror reigned across Stalingrad with street fighting, machine gun fire, and Germans and Russian snipers firing from high-rise buildings. German tanks from the Fourteenth Panzer Division that were patrolling the streets aimed at the next objective of taking the oil-rich Caucasus region. The German Luftwaffe retained air superiority, but struggled to keep troops with fresh supplies because of the Russian's endurance to hold Stalingrad.

When the Sixth Army, commanded by Paulus, reached the Volga region, Stalin had women and children build trenches and replace abandoned positions from fleeing soldiers. Stalin later executed around thirteen thousand soldiers for desertion and cowardice. During the winter months, Russia made a significant turning point when the Red Army began a counter-offensive and launched Operation Uranus. Stalin decided to invade the weaker Romanian and Hungarian forces, which chose to fight for the Axis.

By late November, the Sixty-Second Soviet Army was down but not out. They joined forces near the town of Kalach and advanced just short of Stalingrad. The Red Army was determined to turn the tide of the war and surrounded the city, isolating 220,000 of the German Sixth and portions of the Fourth Army inside Stalingrad.

Hitler had been convinced that his forces would take Stalingrad during the summer months and didn't prepare for a winter campaign. But he was in for a rude awakening - the battle lasted for five and a half grueling months. It was a brutal fight that tested the limits of both sides.

Despite the odds, the Red Army refused to back down. They fought with everything they had to defend their city and push back against the Axis forces.

The German soldiers trapped in Stalingrad not only faced the constant threat of enemy fire but also had to contend with dire living conditions. With no access to much-needed supplies, they were vulnerable to disease, cold weather, and starvation, and most of the population was homeless due to bombing raids and fierce house-to-house fighting. The harsh winter worsened the situation, with temperatures dropping as low as forty degrees below zero. The soldiers struggled to survive, and many succumbed to the brutal conditions.

CHAPTER 7

THE AFTERMATH

The chaos of war has a way of bringing out the best in people, and the Second World War was no exception. As the conflict raged on, the world's greatest thinkers, scientists, and military minds turned their attention to one goal: ending the war as quickly and efficiently as possible. But it wasn't just Allied forces who were working tirelessly to bring an end to the fighting.

Many German scientists had fled Europe during Hitler's conquest of the continent in the 1930s, fearing persecution due to the Nazis' hatred of Jews. The Nuremberg Laws, passed in 1933, forbade employment in the civil service to anyone with a Jewish parent or grandparent - a clear sign that anti-Semitism was on the rise.

Despite this discrimination, many of these brilliant minds found themselves working for Allied forces during the war. Their expertise proved invaluable in developing new technologies and strategies that would ultimately help bring about victory.

It's amazing to think about how even in times of great turmoil and tragedy, humanity can come together to achieve incredible things.

During World War II, the United States was determined to win the race for scientific superiority. To do so, they scoured the globe for the brightest minds in chemistry and physics - including some who had conducted horrific medical experiments on prisoners in Nazi death camps.

A joint intelligence committee was formed to research rockets, jets, biological weapons, and the atomic bomb. The stakes were high, and the pressure was on to develop new technologies that could help bring an end to the war.

One of the most brilliant physicists of the time was none other than Albert Einstein himself. He warned President Franklin Roosevelt of the potential dangers of atomic bombs and urged him to take action. This led to the creation of what would become known as the Manhattan Project - a top-secret government initiative aimed at developing nuclear weapons before Germany could.

The Manhattan Project brought together some of the greatest scientific minds of the time, all working towards a common goal. Their efforts would ultimately lead to the creation of the first atomic bomb - a weapon that would change the course of history forever.

When it comes to the Manhattan Project, Enrico Fermi was one of the key players. As the chief architect at Columbia University in New York, he led a team of brilliant physicists that included the likes of Albert Einstein, Niels Bohr, Leo Szilard, and Robert Oppenheimer.

Together, they worked tirelessly to design and build the first nuclear reactor - a feat that would ultimately lead to the creation of the atomic bomb. But Fermi had bigger dreams than just weapons of destruction. He believed that by controlling the splitting of an atom's nucleus, we could unlock a peaceful means of nuclear power.

Fermi's work on nuclear fission was groundbreaking, and it paved the way for a new era in energy production. But unfortunately, his research was also used to create the atomic bomb - code-named 'Little Boy' - which was dropped on Hiroshima in 1945.

Fermi's legacy lives on today in both our energy production and our understanding of nuclear physics.

When it came to defeating the Axis powers during World War II, the United States knew that they couldn't do it alone. That's why they joined forces with the British in a combined offensive called Operation Pointblank - an intensive aerial bombing campaign over German airspace that began in late January 1943.

The goal of the campaign was simple: to cripple Germany's ability to wage war by targeting their industrial and economic sites. This meant going after everything from U-boat construction yards to factories producing weapons and ammunition.

The Allied offensive campaign was relentless, with coordinated bombing runs taking place around-the-clock from the British Royal Air Force and the United States Army Air Forces. The sheer scale of the operation was staggering, with thousands of planes taking part in each mission.

Despite facing heavy resistance from German anti-aircraft guns and fighter planes, the Allies pressed on. Their efforts paid off in the end, as they were able to severely weaken Germany's ability to wage war and ultimately bring about victory.

The Eastern Front of World War II was one of the most brutal and devastating theaters of the conflict. But on February 2, 1943, the tide began to turn when the Germans' Sixth Army at Stalingrad surrendered to the Russians.

The Nazis were forced to reduce their Luftwaffe flights in combat from Eastern Europe to focus on defending their homeland. But even that wasn't enough to stop the Allies from launching devastating bombing campaigns against German cities.

One such campaign took place in Wuppertal and Hamburg, where combined bombers dropped incendiaries that purposely spread fire, followed by waves of high-explosive bombs. The result was a catastrophic firestorm that killed more than 40,000 people in Hamburg alone.

It's hard to imagine the horror and devastation that war can bring.

When it comes to World War II, there were countless battles and operations that helped turn the tide of the conflict. One such operation was Operation Millennium - the first Thousand Plane Raid launched by the British Royal Air Force in May of 1942.

The target was the German city of Cologne, which was home to numerous industrial sites and airfields. The raid was carried out at night, and it proved devastating - nearly 500 people were killed, with another 45,000-left homeless. The citizens of Cologne were left reeling, with many fleeing the city in the aftermath of the bombing.

The Battle of Midway was another pivotal moment in the war. It began on June 4, 1942 - just six months after the attack on Pearl Harbor. The battle was fought between the United States and Japan, and it proved to be a decisive victory for the Allies.

The battle was fought both in the air and at sea, with both sides suffering heavy losses. But in the end, it was the United States who emerged victorious. The victory at Midway helped turn the tide of the Pacific War and gave Allied forces a much-needed boost in morale.

These events may have taken place decades ago, but their impact is still felt today.

The Battle of Leyte Gulf was one of the most pivotal moments in World War II. It was the largest naval battle in history and it dealt a crippling blow to the imperial Japanese Navy.

But the fighting at Leyte Gulf wasn't just significant because of its size. It was also the first battle in which the Japanese carried out organized kamikaze aircraft and suicide attacks. The desperation of their tactics was a clear sign that they knew they were fighting a losing battle.

Meanwhile, on the European front, Allied forces were gearing up for their largest combined offensive yet. In early January 1944, they launched an all-out assault on German forces, determined to bring an end to the war as quickly as possible.

And while battles raged on across the globe, the Big Three - Roosevelt, Churchill, and Stalin - met in Cairo at the Tehran Conference. They discussed strategy and made plans for how to move forward in the war effort.

It's incredible to think about how much was happening during this time period. When it comes to World War II, the Allies were always looking for new ways to gain the upper hand. That's why they launched Operation Shingle - an amphibious assault on the German Tenth Army defensive positions at Anzio, Italy.

The operation was a massive undertaking, involving infantry, artillery units, tank regiments, and fighter jets. The goal was to surprise the Germans and break through their defenses.

And surprise them they did. The French and British corps were able to break through the Gustav Line from the enemy south of the beachhead, while the US Fifth Army crossed the Rapido River and traveled through the center and north of the port city.

But victory wasn't easy. The Allies faced heavy resistance from German forces, and the fighting was intense. Despite this, they pressed on - determined to achieve their objective.

On January 22, 1944, the Allies were given the command to advance. It was a pivotal moment in the war effort, and it paved the way for even greater victories in the months to come.

The British Fifth and Fifty-Sixth Division launched an attack across the Liri River Valley on the west coast of Italy. Meanwhile, the Thirty-Sixth Infantry Division - a Texas National Guard

Division also known as the Fighting Thirty-Sixth - launched an offensive with the aid of air support and naval gunfire.

Their goal was to tie down German reserves' units in San Pietro, and they did just that. The Germans were so focused on the northern crossing of Anzio that they didn't see this attack coming.

The Fighting Thirty-Sixth proved to be a formidable force, and their bravery and determination helped turn the tide of the war in Italy. They faced heavy resistance from German forces, but they pressed on - determined to achieve their objective.

During World War II, the banks on the German side of the Rapido River were covered with barbed wire, concrete walls, and large trees. This made visibility poor, but it offered protection against Allied forces.

The 141st Infantry Regiment moved toward the Rapido, south of the town of Cassino along the eastern side of the ridge. Meanwhile, the 143rd Infantry Regiment attempted their crossing near Sant'Angelo to attack the heavily fortified town at night.

But as soon as the Germans spotted the infantry units, they unleashed heavy mortar, artillery, and machine gun fire. The battle was intense and brutal, with both sides suffering heavy casualties.

The Allies fought fiercely on the Pacific front to secure Iwo Jima and Okinawa. These islands provided a crucial staging area for attacks on the Japanese main islands.

But the Allies didn't stop there. In November 1944, they unleashed waves of B-29 bombers, dropping incendiary bombs across Japanese and German cities. The result? Cities turned into infernos, with devastating consequences for civilians caught in the crossfire.

Despite this destruction, the enemies were met with a continual flow of newly built ships, tanks, artillery, trucks, jeeps, aircraft, and more. The Allies were determined to win at all costs and they did just that.

On July 16, 1945, the United States successfully tested the atomic bomb creating an enormous mushroom cloud some

40,000 feet high in a remote area of Alamogordo, New Mexico. The code name for this historic event was 'Trinity.'

The blast from the explosion carried more power than twenty thousand tons of TNT and was visible more than two hundred miles away.

Just a few months earlier, all German forces had surrendered unconditionally to the Allies in May 1945. News of the war's end erupted in celebration over Europe, with people dancing in the streets and waving flags.

The Japanese realized that their objective in China could not achieve final victory in the Pacific and East Asia. As a result, they decided to withdraw to the east coast.

But their retreat was not without consequences. The Japanese army abandoned the Japanese colonists who resided in the cities in northern China. Many of these innocent civilians were massacred en route back to Japan.

In response to these atrocities, President Truman issued a request to the Japanese government that they must surrender unconditionally and immediately. Despite this demand, the Allied forces continued to fight fiercely until victory was achieved.

On August 6th, bright and early at 08:15 Hiroshima time, Colonel Paul Warfield Tibbets Jr. piloted the infamous Enola Gay and unleashed the devastating atomic bomb, Little Boy, upon the bustling Japanese army base and industrial city of Hiroshima, with around 350,000 inhabitants. Alongside the *Enola Gay* were two more B-29 aircraft—the Great Artiste for scientific observations and the initially anonymous *Necessary Evil*, led by Captain George Marquardt, responsible for capturing images of the mind-blowing explosion.

Soaring at a staggering altitude of nearly 32,000 feet above Hiroshima, the fission-induced atomic bomb erupted in a jaw-dropping detonation with a force equivalent to over 20,000 tons of TNT, obliterating everything in its path and forever changing history as we know it.

Word spread like wildfire throughout Japan, as Hiroshima continued to burn in the aftermath of the devastating blast. Within moments, a significant portion of its residents, including soldiers, medical staff, and ordinary citizens, had been reduced to ashes by the scorching heat of the explosion. With temperatures reaching a jaw-dropping 7,200°F (3,980°C), blinding waves of radiated heat burst forth at unfathomable speeds, spanning two miles in diameter. A sinister mushroom cloud loomed over the city, unleashing a torrent of radioactive rain and ash upon the beleaguered metropolis. Hiroshima mourned the loss of nearly one hundred thousand souls, with countless more succumbing to the lingering effects of radiation in the months and years that followed.

The atomic bomb dropped on Hiroshima marked a turning point in the war, paving the way for a new chapter in global affairs. Although it resulted in extreme destruction and unimaginable human and environmental consequences, its historical significance cannot be denied. To this day, scholars and policymakers continue to analyze and discuss the event.

On August 8, the Soviets waged war against Japan, launching an assault on the Kwantung Army in a bid to reclaim Manchuria and Korea. With over 1.5 million men, the Red Army's goal was to free China from Japanese rule. Upon arrival, they discovered numerous captives who had been subjected to horrifying experiments.

Faced with the daunting prospect of unconditional surrender, the local population had no choice but to defend themselves against the Soviet invasion alongside the Imperial Japanese Army. When Japan failed to formally announce their surrender, the United States dropped a second atomic bomb, dubbed *"Fat Man,"* on Nagasaki, just three days after unleashing *"Little Boy"* on Hiroshima. A B-29 bomber named Bockscar carried the devastating payload, piloted by Major Charles Sweeney. Upon detonation at 11:02 a.m., Nagasaki time, approximately 40,000 lives were instantly extinguished.

In addition to the appalling acts against the Chinese people, the world became aware of horrifying incidents like rape, murder, and even cannibalism by Japanese soldiers as a means for sustenance. The conflict persisted with the Japanese settlers in Manchuria and China, where the Red Army, too, inflicted similar horrors upon the Chinese and Japanese populations.

Nonetheless, the Soviets offered sympathy and support to the Chinese Communists in their pursuit of foreign foes. They denied access to Nationalist forces in crucial areas near ports and strategic locations. Seizing Japanese equipment in Northeast Asia's Manchuria, the Russians supplied these resources to the Chinese Communist forces.

The clash of ideologies between China's Communist and Nationalist parties escalated into a full-blown civil war shortly after tensions with Japan ceased. This growing conflict amplified the strain between South and North Korea on the Korean Peninsula, eventually leading to the outbreak of the Korean War. Within just a decade, the global conflict between the Axis and Allied powers resulted in a staggering 60 to 80 million fatalities.

This grim chapter of human history, marked by ceaseless civil wars, deception, rampant government corruption, and bloodshed, wiped out nearly 4% of the world's population. Driven by Chiang Kai-shek, the Chinese Nationalists fortified their military presence across the Formosa Strait and established a government on Taiwan's shores, christening it as the Republic of China.

On October 1, 1949, the Chinese Communist Party, under the leadership of Mao Zedong, emerged victorious in the civil war and established the People's Republic of China. Despite efforts by the United States to mediate peace talks between the Nationalists and Communists, the struggle for political liberation persisted across the Pacific and Asia. Gaining support from rural farmers, the Communist parties pledged to combat American forces and formed an alliance with the Soviets.

World War II marked a turning point in establishing a new global order, as discussions unfolded worldwide to create secure borders and promote stability. The goal was to attain world peace by allocating territories among the triumphant leaders who emerged from the war through various peace agreements.

Post-war, Africa saw the reemergence of colonial imperialism, with European powers seizing portions of the vast and mysterious continent. In the Far East, American forces occupied Japan, and Korea was partitioned along the 38th parallel. South of this line, South Korea, supported by the US, became the Republic of Korea. To the north, North Korea emerged as the Democratic People's Republic of Korea under Russia's patronage.

In a display of goodwill, the United States permitted the Japanese emperor to retain his position after becoming the sole occupying force in Japan. With the emperor's intervention, American troops were able to maintain order among the Japanese military with relative ease.

As for the nations allied with the Nazis, they lost their territories following the conclusion of the war. Germany was split into two distinct countries – East Germany, under Soviet control, and West Germany, which adopted a democratic system. Numerous German prisoners of war were subjected to forced labor as a means of making amends, while some of their industries were stripped of resources and technology as war reparations.

During the historic Potsdam Conference, held at Cecilienhof, world leaders gathered to establish peace treaties in the aftermath of war. Germany was split into four separate zones, each controlled by a different Allied force: France in the southwest, Britain in the northwest, the US in the south, and the Soviet Union in the east. As a result, numerous Germans, Japanese, and Arabs were forcibly uprooted from their homes.

During this time, the tense Cold War kicked off, with Germany entangled between the western Allies and the eastern Soviets.

The United States and Britain, eager to promote democracy in their occupied territories, formed a joint governing body.

In the aftermath of World War I, the League of Nations granted Britain the authority to govern Egypt and Palestine under the Treaty of Sevres. Later, in 1936, Britain and Egypt inked the Anglo-Egyptian Treaty, giving Egypt political autonomy in exchange for their support during the First World War. However, it wasn't until July 1956 that the British withdrawal was completed. After World War II, in 1947, the United Nations General Assembly passed a resolution to end British rule in Palestine and divide it into two independent nations – one for Jews and another for Arabs.

On the historic day of May 14, 1948, as the British Mandate for Palestine came to an end, the Jewish council proudly proclaimed the birth of an independent nation - the State of Israel. However, the Arab Higher Committee fiercely opposed this move, igniting a tumultuous civil war and marking the beginning of the infamous Arab/Israeli War of 1948. Both sides targeted British authorities - the Arabs accused them of permitting illegal Jewish settlements in Palestine, while the Jews condemned British-imposed land ownership restrictions.

In the midst of this chaos unfurled a heart-wrenching event: the 1948 Palestinian exodus, or Nakba in Arabic. Between 700,000 and 725,000 Palestinian Arabs were forced to flee their homes seeking safety, while others were driven out by Israeli forces. The United Nations intervened to bring an end to this conflict in 1949. Nevertheless, due to complicated negotiations, a staggering eighty percent of displaced Arab inhabitants were tragically barred from ever returning to their homeland in Palestine.

In 1956, Egypt welcomed the first-ever United Nations peacekeeping force in the Sinai Peninsula, ensuring that all parties adhered to the 1949 Armistice Agreements. Following Israel's frequent cross-border raids that claimed over thirty lives, Egypt struck an arms deal with Russia. Consequently, the United States retaliated by withholding funds for the Aswan Dam project on the Upper Nile River. Meanwhile, resistance against British occupation in Egypt grew significantly as British troops returned to the country.

Egypt's President Nasser called on Great Britain to leave the Canal Zone and imposed a partial blockade on Israel's Red Sea access through Egyptian land. In response, Great Britain, France, and Israel devised a strategy to regain control of the canal and oust Nasser from power. The Suez Canal significantly shortened sea voyages from Europe to Asian markets. Egypt nationalized the Canal Zone to acquire funds and sought assistance from Russia for the Aswan Dam project, turning away from the United States.

On October 29, with the support of Great Britain and France, Israeli forces initiated a surprise strike against Egypt, seizing the Sinai Canal and Gaza Strip. This bold move was orchestrated by the head of the general staff, Moshe Dayan, who successfully claimed the entire Sinai Peninsula from Egyptian control. Subsequently, the British and French militaries invaded and started bombing Cairo to gain control over this crucial waterway.

This chain of events ignited the flames of the historic Six-Day War, or Third Arab-Israeli War, commencing on June 5, 1967. In merely six intense days of combat, Israel captured the Gaza Strip and Sinai Peninsula from Egypt, the West Bank and East Jerusalem from Jordan, and the Golan Heights from Syria. This remarkable feat tripled Israel's land size and was achieved with significant backing from Western allies.

In the aftermath of territorial conquests, millions of Palestinians found themselves living under foreign rule on the West Bank of the Jordan River. The victorious European forces, spearheaded by the British, drastically reshaped the Middle East's political landscape by creating Arab states and asserting a strong influence on local matters.

Post-World War I, Iraq was dominated by Sunni Arabs until Saddam Hussein's regime crumbled following the 2003 United States invasion. This marked the rise of Shia Islam to power – a first since the 17th century – and reestablished Shiite control in Baghdad, Iraq's capital. Consequently, Sunni Arabs found themselves excluded from power.

Following the shift in power, the fresh-faced prime minister vowed to put an end to the endless cycle of revenge between Iraqi Shiites and Sunnis. While the freedom and rise of the Shia-majority population have certainly impacted Iraq and the entire Middle East, it hasn't exactly unfolded the way Western nations predicted. In both Iraq and Syria, numerous Sunni Arabs have found common ground with various ideologies - be it the secular nationalism of the Baath Party, Al-Qaeda, or even ISIS (Islamic State in Iraq and Syria).

In Iraq and Afghanistan, the Sunni branch of Islam has a unique relationship with the Shia branch, which only makes up 10% of the population. In Afghanistan, tribal loyalties are highly valued, resulting in less tension between different Islamic branches. Interestingly, Afghan Muslim clergy, also known as Mullahs, often have jobs as farmers or skilled artisans instead of being part of a formal religious hierarchy.

The Afghan Civil War led to the rise of the notorious Taliban faction, who enforced a strict interpretation of Sharia (Islamic law). Their violent attacks on civilians and discrimination against religious and ethnic minorities drew widespread condemnation. Iran supported the Northern Alliance in their fight against the Taliban regime after they took control of Kabul. The extremist Sunni Islamist group Al-Qaeda and ISI lent their support to the Taliban, intensifying the conflict. As the Taliban gained control, the consequence was a staggering number of nearly two million Afghan refugees.

On October 7, 2001, President George W. Bush revealed that the US had begun airstrikes against Al-Qaeda and the Taliban in

Afghanistan. This action was triggered by the horrific September 11th al-Qaeda suicide attacks. Interestingly, al-Qaeda's roots date back to the Soviet–Afghan War when the Soviet Union invaded Afghanistan from 1979 to 1989.

Fast-forwarding two decades, the Taliban gained control of Afghanistan, imposing their brand of Sunni Islam on the majority of its inhabitants. The striking image of Major General Chris Donahue—the last soldier departing Hamid Karzai International Airport under the cover of darkness—marked the conclusion of America's lengthiest conflict. The Taliban celebrated their victory with spokesman Suhail Shaheen tweeting, "Our country has gained its full independence, praise Allah. Heartfelt congratulations to all countrymen!"

The US intervention in Afghanistan transformed the Afghan way of life, a stark contrast to life under the Taliban. The Taliban were notorious for their human rights violations and strict enforcement of Shariah laws. Since the tragic events of September 11, 2001, where 19 militants launched devastating suicide attacks on New York's World Trade Center and the Pentagon in Arlington, Virginia, claiming nearly 3,000 lives, America has been striving to reshape Afghanistan into a democratic nation.

CHAPTER 8

THE CASTE OF SUPREMACY: THE CAUSES OF ESAU AND JACOB'S CONFLICT IN THE MODERN WORLD

Surprisingly, the intensifying tension in the Middle East and Africa is often attributed to the age-old rivalry between Jacob and Esau, which is said to fuel the ongoing Jewish and Islamic conflicts. In 1946, the Nuremberg war crimes trial brought high-ranking government members to justice, accusing them of igniting World War II.

Since then, Esau morphed into the infamous villain once more, being held responsible for the African/Middle Eastern turmoil. Society has become all too accepting of placing blame, instead of confronting the reality of their government's role in creating global chaos. The sectarian violence between Kurds,

Shiites, and Sunni Arabs in the Middle East has its roots in territorial divisions established by European powers after World War I. These divisions continue to hold a grip on regional governments caught in this relentless conflict.

Political and spiritual figures across the globe have often drawn parallels between their leader's deceitful nature and the character of Esau. This captivating tale opens our eyes to a symbolic reflection of prophetic insight.

The meteoric rise of ISIS has left the Western world in shock, as they defy the borders of Syria and Iraq in pursuit of an Islamic state. Governed by a stringent set of Sharia laws derived from Islam's holy book, the Qur'an, ISIS originated as a radical offshoot of Al-Qaeda. Their ultimate goal is to revive the caliphate, led by a caliph who can trace his lineage back to the Prophet Muhammad. The emergence of these Sunni Islamist militants has sent waves of violence rippling through the region.

The escalating persecution of Christians, Shiites, and Kurds by ISIS has forced them to choose between converting to Sunni Islam or facing execution. The growing influence of this extremist group poses a significant threat to Middle Eastern stability, raising concerns among nations like Israel, Iran, Saudi Arabia, and Turkey.

Meanwhile, the Iranian Women's Rights Movement has bravely challenged the oppressive laws imposed by the Mullahs. These regulations demean women and enforce a rigid caste system. In Iran, men are allowed multiple wives and can legally marry girls as young as nine. Outrage over these injustices boiled over when 22-year-old Masha Amini died in police custody for violating the strict dress code by allegedly not wearing her hijab. This tragedy sparked widespread protests, during which many lost their lives fighting for basic rights and freedom.

The Morality Police in Iran, responsible for enforcing strict dress codes for women, has been disbanded. Protests have erupted not only on the streets of Iran but across the globe. In a show of solidarity, women are cutting their headscarves with teachers and educators joining the uproar through nationwide strikes. These demonstrations have seen hundreds lose their lives in a brave pursuit to eliminate discrimination. Chants echo through the air, proclaiming "With or without hijab, forward to the revolution!" The crowds shout fiercely, "Death to the dictator," "Down with the oppressor, whether Shah or leader Khamenei," and "Our enemy is right here."

In Conclusion, Sudan, a country haunted by civil wars and political instability since its independence from Britain and Egypt in 1956, is also grappling with a deep-rooted caste system. This system stems from the division between the lighter-skinned Arab, Muslim-majority north and the predominantly darker-skinned Christian or traditional faith-following south. It's this divides that has perpetuated a caste hierarchy leading to ongoing conflicts among Africans.

The origin of Sudan's caste system can be traced back to historical and cultural influences by European colonizers. The northern Arabs, lighter-skinned and powerful, have long exercised dominance over the southern darker-skinned Africans. Various economic, social, and political elements have reinforced this imbalance over time.

One crucial aspect was colonial rule when the British favored Sudan's Arab population. They provided access to education and other opportunities denied to the darker African population. This preferential treatment gave rise to a lingering division between the two groups that still exists today – an outcome of the cunning European Invaders' divide-and-conquer strategy.

Further exacerbating the situation is Sudan's history of Arab-led governments that have consistently marginalized African people. This marginalization has fueled resentment among Africans who frequently resort to separatist movements in search of their rights.

Sudan's caste structure is an intricate problem deeply entwined with historical and cultural factors. Tackling this issue demands collective determination from all stakeholders to advocate for equality and justice for every Sudanese citizen while denouncing the caste hierarchy established by European Invaders.

By examining these interconnected issues, it becomes evident that addressing Sudan's caste system and combating racial discrimination worldwide requires collective determination and advocacy for equality and justice. It is crucial for all stakeholders to challenge the historical and cultural factors that perpetuate these inequalities and work towards a more inclusive society.

Ultimately, the history of Sudan serves as a reminder of the importance of understanding our shared history, acknowledging the injustices of the past, and actively striving for a future where all individuals are treated with dignity and respect, regardless of their ethnicity or social background.

Additionally, biblical references delve into the evil of the caste system and shed a light on prophecies and the concept of the day of the Lord. It draws attention to historical events like the countless wars and the transatlantic slave trade, emphasizing their impact on global power dynamics and economic development.

In the intriguing Book of Revelation, we discover a formidable force hailing from the east, sweeping across the Euphrates and advancing westward. This massive army, numbering over 200 million and donning striking red, deep blue, and vibrant yellow armor, will blaze a devastating path through the region. The story unfolds as the sixth angel blows his trumpet, and the apostle John overhears a voice emerging from the four horns of the golden altar near the Lord. The voice commands: "Unleash the four angels bound by the vast Euphrates.

In a fierce battle for control, the powerful Beast described in the Bible will clash with a mighty eastern force over the ancient lands of Africa, the Middle East, Israel, and Palestine. As alliances form across the Middle East, Far East, and Africa, a new world order emerges. In this ominous landscape, demonic spirits strive to seize control of the global economy, forging a world unlike any we've seen before. (Rev 9:13-14).

The epic battle of Armageddon, as strikingly predicted in the book of the prophet Joel, is often referred to as the day of the Lord. This prophecy suggests that a series of natural disasters – floods, fires, storms, and earthquakes – will besiege our planet before the extraordinary day of the Lord unfolds. This climactic battle will precede the arrival of the Messiah. God will employ these natural calamities as a final call for humanity to abandon their wicked ways before His divine anger takes over:

"Let all who dwell on earth shudder; For the day of the Lord draws near, it is upon us: A Day filled with darkness and despair, a day concealed by clouds and impenetrable gloom, much like morning fog engulfing the mountains. A vast and powerful people shall emerge, unlike any that have ever existed; there will never be another like them, even across countless generations" (KJV).

On September 22, 1980, amidst Iran's political chaos caused by the Islamic revolution, Iraq launched a bold invasion on western Iran. Age-old border disputes between the two countries ignited this daring move. Eager to gain the upper hand, Saddam Hussein commanded his troops to conquer the strategically crucial Shatt al-Arab waterway and seize control of Khorramshahr. Additionally, he sought to secure the oil-rich, Arabic-speaking territory of Khuzestan while simultaneously destroying ten Iranian air bases.

Support for Iraq came from powerful nations like the United States and the Soviet Union, along with regional allies like Saudi Arabia and Kuwait. Meanwhile, Iran's key supporters were Syria and Libya. Interestingly, before the conflict ended, the United States played a double game by also selling arms to Iran through Israel's government, leading to the infamous Iran-Contra Affair.

In 1985, the Reagan Administration covertly agreed to supply arms to Iran to help free American hostages detained by terrorists in Lebanon. The Iran/Iraq War persisted from September 1980 until a ceasefire was signed in 1988, resulting in over a million lives lost. The Euphrates River will serve as a central battleground for numerous conflicts led by the antichrist to challenge the authority of God.

Throughout history, power often resided in the hands of those who sought supremacy. Individuals tend to revel in the freedom to commit evil acts, as long as they perceive moral righteousness on their side. They always strive to be right, even when their actions are wrong. Possessing dominance grants them absolute power and the ability to manipulate historical events in their favor. As the saying goes, "Victors write history," suggesting that much of our recorded history may not accurately represent the truth. The quest for supremacy is steering humanity towards a fiery abyss.

In today's world, Esau's tainted image symbolizes our frailty and struggle to face the harsh truth. Esau, a man known for his outdoor prowess, became a skilled hunter with rugged values and a fondness for foreign women. He didn't place much importance on his spiritual legacy. Jacob cleverly offered Esau a bowl of stew in return for his birthright and later used deceit to secure their father's blessing meant for Esau, the firstborn.

The trickery was so blatant that it's hard to miss the significance of the Lord's covenant. Nevertheless, with God's blessing rooted within him, Esau inherited greater wealth than Jacob. The descendants of Jacob and Esau have been blessed with the heavenly dew and the riches of the earth, a fortune that continues to be enjoyed by many Afro-Asiatic people today.

Africa's immense riches and the quest for oil in the Middle East have been crucial to the industrial growth of Europe and America, even influencing both world wars. There's no end to the lengths outsiders will go to seize resources and wealth from the Afro-Asiatic people, leaving them with unthinkable hardships in return.

Throughout Africa and the Afro-Asiatic region, the entire Cushite territory received abundant agricultural blessings. However, the most significant gifts for the descendants of Jacob were spiritual ones yet to come. Both Jacob's and Esau's descendants fed the known world through resilient, productive agriculture.

The entire globe has been graced by the influential Hebrew tribe of Africa and their Jewish kin who revitalized Europe in its darkest times and enriched the Americas with their abundance of natural resources and tireless work ethic. As the transatlantic slave trade brought Africans to the Americas, a rich variety of crops followed in their wake. Staple foods like the Kola nut (an original ingredient in Coca-Cola), peanuts, bananas, black-eyed peas, kidney beans, lima beans, yams, watermelons, and okra accompanied the enslaved individuals on their harrowing journey.

Over time, an assortment of fruits, vegetables, and grains from Africa, accompanied by forced laborers, transformed significant parts of Europe and the Americas into a global food haven. This abundance of food, resources, and economic prosperity set the stage for America to rise as the world's leading power. It's important to remember that to avoid annihilation, the Ten Tribes of Israel and numerous Judeans from Asia Minor and the Aegean Islands fled to North and Central Africa. A large number settled in West Africa where they could live in safety, before the transatlantic slave trade. Wielding a sword and whip, the key to dominating a population lies in weaving countless lies. The web of deception goes on unendingly.

In the ancient text of Revelation's Apocalypse, a profound message was sent to the seven churches located along the Aegean coast in Asia Minor under Roman rule. John the Revelator delivered an eye-opening warning from the heavens to the Indigenous people suffering from Roman oppression. He said, "I know your struggles, hardships, and poverty, but you are wealthy in spirit..."

But the perils didn't stop at the Romans' cruel control. The Indigenous people of Asia Minor had lost touch with their ancestral traditions and culture, allowing their riches to be drained away by worshipping Roman and Greek gods.

The civil rights movement and global protests following the two world wars served as powerful catalysts, compelling individuals to confront their own racial and political biases. The Western world had previously rationalized the bloodshed on streets and battlefields by highlighting the atrocities of the Nazi regime, claiming a moral responsibility to engage in necessary violence. Both Axis and Allied forces shared the blame for the destruction and loss of life during this dark time in history. Concurrently, other regions of the world also witnessed horrific acts as nations battled for control over God-given boarders.

The concept of distinguishing between the Axis' brutal death camps and the strategies of suppressing lesser nations had subtly emerged in the consciousness of American and European communities. With a biased viewpoint on human lives, the world witnessed entire cultures being uprooted for materialistic and self-serving pursuits. Similarly, in today's Christian world, the struggle between Esau and Jacob became more justified.

History books mustn't gloss over the brutal and racist attitudes that have spread worldwide. The Germans harbored intense hatred for Jews and people of African descent, and each European nation devised its own strategy to acquire land and resources. In reality, racism and greed were the driving forces behind both world wars. Not even biblical prophecies seem to influence the sinister or naive attempts to downplay historic occurrences.

European imperialists justified their harsh actions by claiming their superior Anglo-Saxon culture had a moral duty to improve the lives of those considered lesser. They aimed to raise others' cultural standards and instill a reverence for their version to worship "whiteness."

In one stroke, the status of African women who once held significance was diminished to that of second-class citizens under the European caste system. An intentional tension was created by the ruling class to divide and conquer the native population, making it increasingly challenging for them to make ends meet. This new ideology of the rulers shut the doors of equality and wreaked havoc on social institutions at every stage of development. No matter their gender, Africans were burdened with the relentless task of constructing colonial empires throughout the former Cushite lands.

The Nazis' hateful actions towards Jews were a key factor in justifying the fight against the Axis powers. Hitler used the myth of Aryan supremacy to rationalize the mass murder and cruel experiments on Jewish people. Both Jews and Gypsies were accused of impurity, having a mixture of African blood leading to their systematic capture and brutal treatment in concentration camps where they were executed, burned, or forced into extreme labor.

Hitler was a firm believer in the ancient notion of Aryanism and white superiority, which led him to annihilate the black power base through genocide. In contrast, the rest of Europe adopted a more contemporary approach to suppress people of African descent by economically manipulating them, thus boosting capitalism. This method of subjugation paved the way for Western Europe and the United States to excel in both technological advancements and social economics.

In essence, those with even a hint of African heritage were often oppressed and deemed inferior. European imperialism further curtailed the freedom of Africans, subjecting them to mental and physical torment without any acknowledgement of their suffering. Europeans labeled this brutal treatment as the "noble savage," comparing it to the discrimination faced by India's untouchables. In their own homeland, Africans experienced cruel manipulation and devastation. The Anglo-Saxons' belief in their divine right to rule and reference to sacred history minimized the importance of the atrocities committed against the African people.

The fascinating book of Daniel reveals the fierce actions of four powerful gentile kingdoms, starting with Babylon and ending with the Roman Empire. This gripping tale weaves together the story of ten divisions emerging from Rome's collapse, foretelling their reign over the world until the arrival of the Messiah to establish His earthly domain. Throughout history, echoes of the Roman Empire's influence consistently resurface as European nations battle for global supremacy.

Throughout the post-war period, the horrors of the two world wars exposed the atrocities committed by the Nazi regime against innocent civilians. Regrettably, many accounts overlook the devastating impact on indigenous Africans, whose lands were seized and suffered far more significant losses. These people were often dismissed as mere casualties.

During both world wars, the untold suffering of innumerable African lives in the dark chapter of the "black holocaust" casts a lingering memory. Their cries for justice continue to resonate, and as humans, we must overcome the oppressive chain of superiority. Embracing and acknowledging this tormented past can pave the way for healing and growth within our shared history.

A divide exists between the secular view of history and our inherent desire to ascend from mere material pursuits to a divine level of greatness. Unfortunately, this spiritual disconnect has led to the acceptance of wrongdoing as a means to quickly gain wealth, often resulting in prejudice, hostility, and the mistreatment of individuals due to their race or ethnicity throughout history.

In reality, elitism has led many people away from the virtuous path, causing them to adopt a twisted version of worship influenced by Lucifer and his fallen angels. These wicked beings revealed secret knowledge to their early followers. The amazing symbolism of the evergreen tree, representing devotion to these fallen angels, highlights humanity's constant attachment to a materialistic world crafted by Lucifer and his dark forces. Then, in a dramatic turn of events, Yeshua the Christ returns to break apart this complex system created through the collaboration of malevolent spiritual leaders who have dared to defy God Almighty.

How you are fallen from heaven, O Lucifer, son of the morning! How you are cut down to the ground, you who weakened the nations! For you have said in your heart: "I will ascend into heaven, I will exalt my throne above the stars of God; I will also sit on the mount of the congregation on the farthest sides of the north; I will ascend above the heights of the clouds, I will be like the Highest." Yet you shall be brought down to Sheol, to the lowest depths of the Pit. Those who see you will gaze at you, and consider you, saying: "Is this the man who made the earth tremble, who shook kingdoms, who made the world a wilderness and destroyed cities, who did not open the house of his prisoners?"

(Isa. 14:12–7)

CONCLUSION

The Journey of the Israelites and the descendants of Esau have been severe, with a balancing act to maintain freedom and a greater loyalty to worship God.

The result is the hierarchy of white male dominance fighting to maintain absolute power and wage a revolutionary war against its rivals to protect the status quo. Since the old days, freedom has constantly been interrupted by insatiable greed and the consequences of the fear of losing power to preserve dominance over theft. In essence, fostering equality and embracing forgiveness means finding common ground with those who have wronged us and striving to transform the hearts of our adversaries.

In the Western world, White Christian nationalists have found common ground with White supremacists. The unsettling notion of losing their privileged status drives their belief system, which is tied to justifying European colonization. White nationalism has always prioritized power and greed over true devotion to our Creator.

In Iran, an uproar has erupted as men and women take to the streets, protesting the tragic death of Mahsa Amini. She lost her life after being detained by the nation's morality police for not wearing her hijab properly. Shockingly, she was allegedly assaulted by Iranian authorities, leading to a coma, and ultimately her death three days later.

The fierce fight for Islamic feminism is currently waging against the entrenched power of male chauvinism. As a critical component of a broader global feminist movement, Islamic feminism strives to dethrone this oppressive power, striving for total equality and social justice for everyone—both Muslims and non-Muslims—within a unified feminist movement.

In a fiery display of defiance, women are burning their headscarves in protest against gender-based violence and discrimination, causing ripples of unease throughout the nation. Jessica Chastain, a prominent actress, draws a striking comparison between Iran and Ukraine, asserting that Ukraine garners more attention due to its predominantly white population. Chastain points out the double standard surrounding coverage of the Iranian women's uprising as she shares her experiences with the press: "I've done a lot of press recently, and many people want to talk about Ukraine. But when I bring up Iran, no one wants to talk about that."

In summary, the threat to democracy and the rapid changes in teaching history to a younger generation is becoming just as controversial as our struggle for equality. Yeshua Ha'Mashiach, aka Jesus Christ, brought a new love movement and equilibrium. The sad thing was that the gentiles who immigrated to Israel and Palestine threatened to throw Christ over a cliff.

Yeshua Ha'Mashiach (Jesus Christ) was born in Bethlehem, Palestine – South of Jerusalem, in a manger, a gutter where animals eat. Bloodshed was the norm for dark skin Palestinians and Israelites living in the Promised Land. This was true throughout the region with White Supremacists and the Romans' way of life that was not going to show any mercy, even for the genocide of killing young black infants.

The freedom to empower our children to the truth of past atrocities committed against people of color is still a threat to White Superiority and Supremacy.

BIBLIOGRAPHY

About Education. Madagascar Plan. http://history 1900s. about.com/od/ holocaust/a/madagascarplan 2.htm.

The Atlantic Photo. World War II: After the War. Article published October30, 2011.http://www.theatlantic.com/ photo/2011/10/world-war-ii-after-the-war/100180/.

Appleby, Joyce, Lynn Hunt, and Margaret Jacob. *Telling the Truth about History*. New York: W. W. Norton & Company, 1994.

Barberet, D. *In Abraham and Sarah*. Broomall: Mason Crest Publishers, 2009.

Beevor, A. *The Second World War*. New York: Little, Brown and Company Hachette Book Group, 2012.

Benson, C. *Supernatural Dreams and Visions*. Plainfield: Logos International, 1970.

Burton, K. A. *The Blessing of Africa: The Bible and African Christianity*. Downers Grove: InterVarsity Press, 2007.

Carter, J. *Palestine Peace Not Apartheid*. New York: Simon & Schuster, 2006.

Ciment, J. *Atlas of African American History*. New York: Checkmark Books, 2001.

Cummins, J. *The World's Bloodiest History*. Beverly: Fair Winds Press, 2010.

Harry S. Truman Library and Museum. "Atomic Bomb- Truman Press Release." www.trumanlibrary.org/ teacher/abomb.htm, August 6, 1945.

Haskew, Michael. *The World War II Desk Reference: Eisenhower Center for Americans Studies*. New York: Grand Central Press, 2004.

Hazleton, L. *Jezebel: The Untold Story of the Bible's Harlot Queen*. New York: Doubleday, 2007.

Heale, Jay, and Jui L. Young. *Cultures of the World: Democratic Republic of the Congo*. Tarrytown: Times Publishing Limited, 2010.

Hillel, D. *In the Natural History of the Bible*. New York: Columbia University Press, 2006.

History Learning Site. Retrieved from "Jews in Nazi Germany." http://www.historylearningsite.co.uk/Jews Nazi Germany.htm.

Hoak, B. T. *Jacob*. Broomall: Manson Crest Publishers, 2009.

Naval History and Heritage Command. "Shangri-La." www.history.navy.mil/danfs/s11/shangri-la.htm.

Nishi, D. *Life during the Great Depression*. San Diego: Lucent Books, 1998.

Olson, Todd. *Leopard II: Butcher of the Congo (A Wicked History)*. New York: Scholastic, Inc.

The Oxford Companion to World War II. Oxford: Oxford University Press, 1995.

Readers Digest: Atlas of the Bible. Pleasantville: The Reader's Digest Association, 1981.

Resnick, A. *The Holocaust*. Lincoln: Lucent Books, 1991. Spiegel, M. *The Dreaded Comparison: Human and Animal*

Slavery. New York: Mirror Books, 1996.

Thomas Nelson Publishers. The Holy Bible, New King James Version, 1992

The Tower. "The Map that Ruined the Middle East." Article published. www.thetower.org/article/the-map- that-ruined-the-middle-east, July 2013

Uschan, M. V. *The 1910s*. San Diego: Lucent Books, 1999.

Vaughan, D. *The Everything World War II Book*. Avon: Adams Media Corporation, 2002.

Wagner, H. L. *The Division of the Middle East: The Treaty of Sevres*. Philadelphia: Chelsea House Publishers, 2004.

Wilson, A. N. *Paul: The Mind of the Apostle*. New York: W. W. Norton & Company, 1997.

Spiegel, Marjorie. *The Dreaded Comparison: Human and Animal Slavery*. New York: Mirror Books, 1996.

Wikipedia. "Atomic bombings of Hiroshima and Nagasaki." en.wikipedia.org/wiki/Atomic bombings_ of Hiroshima and Nagasaki.

Wikipedia. "Doolittle Raid." en.wikipedia.org/wiki/ Doolittle Raid.

Wikipedia. "Operation Shingle." en.wikipedia.org/wiki/ Operation Shingle.

Internet Sources:

The New York Times. Millions of Armenians Killed or in Exile: www.armeniapedia.org/wiki/Million Armenians Killed or In Exile, 1915, December 15

The New York Times. Thousands Protest Armenian Murders: www.armeniaapedia.org/wiki/Thousands Protest Armenians Murders, 1915, October

Hitler's Forgotten Black victims. Hitler's black victim. http://www.daveyd.com/hitlerpol.html, 1967,

September 26

Wikipedia, the free encyclopedia. Six-Day War: en.wikipedia.org/wiki/Six-Day War, 2000

Doolittle Raid. The Mission and the Man. www.national- museum.af.mill/factsheets/factsheet.asp, 2011, February 4

Announcing the Bombing of Hiroshima Other Primary Resources. www.pbs.org/.../features/primary-resources/ Truman Hiroshima, August 6, 1945

Athenaeum Library of Philosophy. Heidegger's Racialist Friend: evans-experientialism.freewebspace.com/ eugen-fischer.htm

Himba People. en.wikipedia.org/wiki/Himba People Shangri-La. Wikipedia: en.wikipedia.org/wiki/Shangri-La Iran-Iraq War. Wikipedia,thefreeencyclopedia.1988http://en.wikipedia.org/wiki/Iran%E2%80%93Iraq War, 22 September 1980 – 20 August 1988

Iran-Iraq War. http://www.globalsecurity.org/military/ world/war/iran-iraq.htm, 1980-1988

Iran-Iraq War. Britannica Online Encyclopedia. http:// www.britannica.com, 1980-88

All Bible scripture references are from The New King James Version published by Thomas Nelson Publishers, Inc., 1992

www.ingramcontent.com/pod-product-compliance
Lightning Source LLC
Chambersburg PA
CBHW020655060526
44119CB00068B/17